Heaven Spoke

I HAVE BEEN WAITING FOR YOU FOR SO LONG!

MEI LI BREAKWELL

Heaven Spoke
I Have Been Waiting For You For So Long!
by Mei Li Breakwell

Printed in the United States of America

Edited by Xulon Press

ISBN 9781498419260

Unless otherwise indicated, Scripture.quotations are taken from the HOLY BIBLE, NEW INTERNATIONAL VERSION. Copyright 1973, 1978, 1984 by International Bible Society. Used by permission of Zondervan Publishing House.

Flowers of the Field, used by permission, ORTV, Heavenly Melody, Taipei, Taiwan, 1980. ORTV Heavenly Melody TEL+886-2-2533-9123 / FAX+886-2-2533-0606 / Address#10, Lane 62, Dazhi Street, Taipei 10462,Taiwan

www.xulonpress.com

ACKNOWLEDGMENTS

My most grateful thanks to all who gave me help on writing this manuscript. My special thanks go to: Graham Breakwell, Valerie Segura, Charlie Segura, Hazel Harken, Douglas Cannon, Grant Goble, Chris Doyle, Barbara Davidson, Alice Song, Jeff Plumley, John Lambert, Stephen Mbogo.

TABLE OF CONTENTS

Part Three: Recalling My Past

Part Four: New Life In Jesus Christ

INTRODUCTION

This is a true story. It's not about me but about Jesus Christ. I have to share it because this story belongs to everyone in this world. Although I am in the story, I am not the important person. What is essential is what I saw, heard, and experienced that transformed my life forever. I pray that you, my readers, may have an encounter with Jesus Christ, and accept what I accepted, be transformed in the way I was transformed, and look forward to what I am looking forward to—eternal life with Jesus.

I was born into a family of three in June of 1969. My parents and my older sister lived in a small town by the Yangzi River in Chongqing, China. While growing up, I was educated to be an atheist. I had neither heard the Christian message nor ever believed in the existence of God. Whenever I heard a life after death story in which a person went to heaven, I would always think it was a ridiculous fantasy.

When I was a teenage girl, I became very rebellious. I disliked school, slept in classes, and failed exams. I hated my parents' discipline and sometimes ran away from home. I thought my parents didn't love me because I was an adopted child. In pursuit of freedom from their supervision, I got married to a man against their wishes soon after I finished high school.

When my daughter was born, my husband left us in the hospital. My parents took my baby and me back to their home. My heart was broken, and I began to consider God's existence. After my divorce, I was lonely and empty, and my life went in a wrong direction. I went to Hainan Island for a vacation with a married man. On this trip, a sudden danger rose when I was standing in the ocean. While I was waiting to die, someone came from above and showed me everything that I had done in my life and saved me, yet I didn't know who He was at the time. After I left the island, I started a journey to find out His name. I later discovered that it was Jesus who had appeared to me. This amazing miracle and unforgettable experience completely changed all that I had believed about life. I was converted from an atheist to a Christian.

Over the next seventeen years whenever I tried to speak or write down this story, I would stutter or tremble. Finally, the Holy Spirit inspired me and enabled me to write down this story so that others can come to know Jesus Christ and put their faith in Him. I hope all who read this story are moved by the Almighty God and give all the glory and thanks to Christ my Savior.

My dear friend, please follow me now. Let me take you back to that hot summer many years ago. For some, it may seem like the distant past, but for me it is as if it were yesterday.

THE HEAVEN OF MY DREAMS

Someone once asked me, "What is your biggest dream?" I answered without any hesitation, "To see the ocean!" He responded with great surprise, "See the ocean? That's all? Can you tell me why?" I smiled at him and said, "It's a secret." There were certain things that I wanted to keep only for myself.

I grew up in inland China by the Yangtze River. I had never seen the ocean, but I had often heard people say how vast it was and how much unlimited mystery it contained, so I always dreamed about it. During my childhood, I often blended what I had read in books and had seen in movies, and I would close my eyes and imagine the ocean—the blue sky, flying seagulls, golden beach, lines of footprints, low and high tides, surging waves, white spray, playing children, and joyful smiles. In my heart, the ocean was the most beautiful place in the world, and it was the heaven of my dreams.

I often asked myself why could the ocean make lovers more passionate, the lonely feel cared for, and the despairing become hopeful. Why could the ocean heal the pain of the sufferer, calm the temper of the angry, and comfort the homesick? Why did the ocean contain such a mysterious power that could give anyone a new beginning?

Somehow my intuition told me that many questions about life could be answered if I could go to the ocean. That's why I had longed for it and had waited to see it ever since I was a little girl. I thought I could die without any regrets if I could just see the ocean even once in my lifetime. I didn't think that the day would ever arrive, nor did I imagine that it would change my life so completely.

The end of July 1996 marked the second year after my divorce. At this same time I graduated from Chengdu University of Traditional Chinese Medicine with an associate degree. My boyfriend Bert, a German fellow with blue eyes, came from Germany to visit me in Chengdu. He was going to take me to Sanya on Hainan Island for a vacation. I would finally see the ocean, the heaven of my dreams, at the southernmost tip of China. We planned to stay in Sanya for seven days.

I had just turned 27 years old that year. I was young and a complete atheist. Like millions of other Chinese people, I was taught in school that human beings evolved from monkeys and that there had never been a God of creation or a Savior of this world. I totally believed that there was no God, nor were there things like spirits, angels, devils, heaven, or hell. In the little town where I lived for more than twenty-five years, I had never seen a church building, knew a book called the Bible, or heard a story about Jesus Christ. All I had was a belief that I could conquer anything and get what I wanted if I put enough effort into it. I believed that I was the one in charge of my life and in control of my fate.

With such a belief, I stepped onto the airplane with Bert. We flew from Chengdu to Haikou in a regular aircraft, and then from Haikou to Sanya in a small airplane. When we took off from Haikou Airport, I saw that the only passengers on the airplane were Bert and I. The rest of the seats were empty. It was as if Bert had hired a private plane just for our vacation. I thought to myself, *How wonderful! What a romantic beginning of this trip! How unforgettable! The seven days that we are going to spend in Sanya must be as special as this plane ride*. I was so excited and looking forward to the place where we were flying.

As the plane passed through the sky over Hainan Island, I looked down. I didn't know what I would see, hear, and experience in the heaven of my dreams, but I had made a promise to myself: I would warmly embrace every day. I would cherish every moment. I would engrave the memory in my mind and enshrine it forever.

After arriving in Sanya and checking into the hotel, Bert and I put on swimsuits and slippers and applied sunscreen. We took a camera, our sunglasses, and our bath towels. Bert hung a small cylinder around his neck before leaving the room. He tightened the top after putting some money into it to make sure that the water would not get into it. If we became hungry or thirsty later, we could use the money to buy something to eat or drink. Then we walked out of the room and headed toward Da Dong Hai Beach, the most famous beach in Sanya.

It was a great surprise for me that there were so few people on the airplane, but there were so many people on the beach. Bert laid our bath towels on the sandy beach. He sat down and asked me to do the same. He suggested that we enjoy the sunshine first and relax ourselves before going into the water, but I could hardly wait. I was going to race toward the ocean. I wanted to sink myself into its arms. I wanted to be kissed by it. I wanted to feel its strength. I had waited for this moment for so many years. My dream finally came true, and the happiness that I had longed for was right there. I wanted to grab it, hold it tight, and keep it before it slipping away.

Bert stopped me. He hung the camera around his neck and took many pictures capturing the moment I approached the ocean for the first time of my life. After taking many photos from different angles, he let me head for the ocean. I quickly crossed the soft, hot sand and stepped in the water. I felt the heat rise from the bottom of my feet, gentle, warm, and comfortable. I eagerly walked toward the deeper water, but the surging waves, one after another, formed a fair amount of resistance. It slowed my advance. With great difficulty, I managed to walk to where the water reached my waist.

I stopped and looked to the left and to the right. Two men were about even with me. They were both strong, middle-aged men and were only two feet away. Suddenly, an idea from nowhere flashed through my mind: *I am safe here, such a small distance from them. If something happens, they can help me when I cry out. Great!* I was very satisfied with my arrangement, feeling safe around these two men.

Facing the open sea, I stretched out my arms, closed my eyes, and drew a deep breath. Each sound of the sea filled my ears. The hot sea breeze brushed my face smelling moist and fresh. To me, this smell was cordial and familiar, as if I had been born near the ocean and grew up surrounded by its scent. It was as if I had never lived without it. It was as if my life were completely blended in with it, as if the only reason that I had come was for this smell.

I finally exhaled the sea air after letting it linger in my chest for a long time. Then I opened my eyes and took in the enormous panoramic view. The endless sea was wide open in front of me. This was the heaven of my dreams! The sky above me was azure blue. A few white clouds were floating in the sky like cotton balls, and under the sky the sea was like a deep blue sapphire. The other end of the sea disappeared into the horizon. I was amazed by the vastness and extensiveness of the sea. It was just how people described it. What a beautiful, peaceful and perfect view.

I watched it, fascinated, and thought, *Is this the end of the earth? Is this where the sun rises every day?* It was the first time I had seen and felt the sea, but I didn't know why there was a very special feeling rising from inside me, a feeling like a wanderer coming back to her mother and finding her dependency and her destiny. That feeling comforted me and made me want to cry.

Whoosh, whoosh. The sound of the waves resonated in my ears. The motion of the waves moved my body forward and backward. I stood there quietly and let the hot sun burn down on my skin. Facing the broad sea, I realized how small I was. I was even smaller than just a drop of the sea. I wanted to relax, but I couldn't. The excitement that I felt when I first saw the sea gradually disappeared. I began to feel emotionally exhausted, helpless, and even useless. I was usually a happy person smiling in front of other people, but at this moment I could no longer smile. I was the only one who knew the bitterness in my heart.

As I looked out at the sea I began to question things in my life. *Why is life so unfair? Those people on the beach are worry-free and happy. They enjoy their lives thoroughly, but I am young and already divorced. I depend on a small salary around twenty dollars per month from the pharmaceutical factory where I work. My salary is not even enough to buy drinking water for my three-year-old daughter. How can I raise her up by myself? I am on leave without pay. My factory sent me to a university for postgraduate study and now I have graduated. Should I stay in Chengdu to look for a new job, or should I go back to my hometown and continue to work at the same factory? I am a divorced woman, and who will marry me? How can I spend my time without a man to rely on in the future? This man Bert has a wife and children. He will never marry me, and I cannot depend on him. What can I do?*

Standing in the ocean, those worries, like a heavy burden, pressed upon my heart making me stressed. I felt like I could hardly breathe. I was inconsolable, and I felt that I had no alternatives in life. This sad feeling replaced the joy of seeing the sea for the first time of my life. I felt frightened and hopeless. I thought of my three-year-old daughter who was living with my parents in my hometown. Her beautiful smiling face flashed in my mind. It reminded me of how much I loved her and how much she relied on me. That helped me gain a little bit of strength.

When I thought that I couldn't give my daughter a complete family, I was in great pain. I wanted to cry. Tears filled my eyes, but I had to force them back. There were many people on the beach, and it would have been embarrassing if they saw me. My heart was exhausted. Standing in the heaven of my dreams, I felt my road had come to an end. What could I do? I had no idea. A long sigh came from the bottom of my heart. "Ay, who can help me?"

Chapter 2

I WALKED THROUGH
THE VALLEY OF DEATH

Suddenly I woke up from my daydreaming. I realized my feet were not standing on the bottom, and my body was floating in the sea. I stretched out my feet wondering how deep the water was, but my big toes could barely touch the sand. When I realized my situation, I started to swim toward the shore. As I was swimming back, I thought to myself, *I learned how to swim in the Yangtze River when I was nine years old. Even the big waves in the river never frightened me. Such a short distance from here to the shore should be simple enough. I can easily get back to the beach.* But it was very strange. I wasn't getting any closer to the shore. On the contrary, I was floating farther away.

I was a little bit afraid and started to swim more seriously. But why did it seem like people on the beach were becoming smaller? I became very frightened and tried with all my might to swim back. At that moment, I could feel very clearly that beneath the water something like two hands were holding my ankles firmly and dragging me down into the water. The more I struggled, the tighter they held me and the more they pulled me down.

I was not strong enough to get away from the hands. Suddenly I understood that I was in the valley of death, and horror overwhelmed me. I thought to myself, *I haven't paid my last respects to my parents yet. I haven't said goodbye to my daughter. They don't even know where I am. They will look for me if I disappear like this. They will go crazy if they can't find me. No, I cannot die. I cannot!* My mind was whirring rapidly.

My eyes quickly glanced at the shore. I was hoping Bert would see my dangerous situation and run to save me. But how could I pick him out from so many people standing on the beach? How could he see me with so many swimmers spread out in the shallow parts of the water? In the crowd, no one cared about my existence. No one was watching me. No one knew of my panic.

I had been in line with the two men standing on my left and on my right in the water, but now I was being pulled away from the shore and from them. I was so anxious, and I started to cry. The urge to survive drove me to ask for help from the man on my left. I looked at him and staked all my hopes on him. With all of my heart and soul I wanted to cry out to him, "Help, help!"

The hands under the water had already moved up to my throat before I could cry out. I realized at this moment that an invisible power was trying to kill me and I became extremely frightened. The hands choked me and my voice was stuck in my throat. I could not make any noise. The man in the water next to me turned his face to me. He looked at my lips, which were moving. No sound came out, so he just smiled at me and then turned his face away as if he saw nothing.

In great fear, I instantly turned my face to the man on the right. *Help! Help!* I wanted to say. The hands held my throat even tighter. I felt like I was suffocating, and I could not make any noise at all. My lips were moving and trying to shout, Help! Help! But no sounds came out. My throat was totally sealed by the hands. The man looked at me and then turned away just like the other man had done.

I didn't understand. How could they all act as if they were blind? Why couldn't they see the hands? Why couldn't they understand my terrified face? Why couldn't they read the message from my eyes begging for life? Why couldn't they know that I was in such danger? I was going to die! They weren't going to save me, and I was dying. I was terrified, but I would not give up. I was driven to stay alive for both my parents and my daughter. I continued to fight. My legs were swinging under the water to support my body. My hands tried to pull away the hands that were holding my throat. However, it was useless. They were so powerful. They held my throat and would not let go.

An idea flashed into my mind. *I'm a goner today! The two men closest to me can't even hear me. If they can't save me, how can I expect those on the shore to help me?* I waved my arms frantically and swatted the water in panic, but my actions were in vain. I could not save myself. My body was turning around and around in the water. The foreign hands moved down to my feet, held my ankles tightly, and with great strength pulled me down toward the bottom of the sea.

My body started to sink. The seawater came above to my chest and then my neck and lips. It forced its way into my mouth, and I had to swallow it. It was bitter, salty, and pungent. I had never drank such terrible tasting water. The seawater continued to rise, and I desperately turned up my face to make sure I could still breathe through my nose. Nevertheless, my nose took in water; I choked and began to flail my arms.

"Is anyone there who can help me?" I cried out from my soul. I was young and had never thought about dying. I didn't want to die, but I was facing death. In the last second of my life, I suddenly felt extremely regretful. I thought to myself, *Life is a gift. How beautiful it is. How worthy it is of being held onto. How good it is to be alive. But life is too short. It was granted to me when I was born, but I didn't treasure it. I have wasted my whole life. If I could live it over again, I would change my lifestyle and live meaningfully.*

At that point, I realized that I was not in charge of my life. It was no longer in my hands. I was helpless. I could not save myself. At that moment, I wished that I could have one more day, a quarter of an hour even, or just a chance to say goodbye to my parents and my daughter, but it was too late. My time was up; I was about to leave this world.

The sea separated me from the world that I knew. The water around me was higher than my head now. No one was around me except the seawater. I was pulled into the lowest point of the wave, and felt like I was going into a bottomless pit. I knew if I was pulled down there, I could never get out. Right then, a big wave came over. A huge face appeared on the peak of that wave. Instantly, I knew it was the face of the devil. The devil had a blue and green face, just like those I had often seen in Buddhist temples. He had two stunted horns on his head, a hideous face, turned up nostrils, and big round eyes bulging out of his face. He looked at me enraged, fierce, and vicious.

He extended his huge, sharp hands that looked like the talons of a large grotesque bird. Riding with the wave, he came at me triumphantly as if I was his prey. He sneered at me and roared, "I am going to destroy you today!" The voice was sinister and manic, filled with desire to devour me. I felt the cords of hell winding around me and pulling me into the pit. I was horrified. My whole body lost strength.

With a great feeling of guilt about my family, I said goodbye to them in my mind: *Mom, Dad, Wei Wei (my daughter), I am so sorry!* After that, I stretched out my arms, and gave up the struggle. Then I closed my eyes and waited for the devil to seize me. I had no choice but to wait to die.

Suddenly, at that very moment, two words blurted out of my mouth without knowing why, "My God!" Instantly, a miracle happened in a way that no one could ever have imagined.

Chapter 3

HE SHOWED ME EVERYTHING
I EVER DID

After I cried out to God, I experienced something that is difficult to explain. At that moment it was as if I was no longer in the ocean. What I believe now is that I entered into the spiritual realm, which I had never believed existed before, and encountered something that I would never forget for the rest of my life. I found myself standing in a spacious place with no one else around. I asked myself, "What kind of place is this? Where am I?" As I was wondering, a powerful vision appeared before my eyes and I became fixed on it.

I saw heaven open, a living object that I had never seen before hovered in the sky. It formed a large thick cloud that quickly came upon me and covered me. I felt a sudden gust of wind and I could hardly stand up. A strong bright light came with the living object and

I was not able to open my eyes, so I lifted up my arms in front of me and watched the sky through my squinting eyes.

As this living object came closer to me, I saw it had a form like a great bird, which was folding its open wings and coming toward me. "The Holy Spirit!" I exclaimed without understanding what I was saying. He landed slowly in front of me. He folded His wings and began to turn Himself rapidly in a counter-clockwise direction. He then became an upright pillar of cloud, bigger on the top and smaller at the bottom. Finally, He assumed the image of a man, and He stood before me.

Who is He? I thought to myself. Before I understood what was going on, I saw some images emerged. They were short and kind natured. They had human forms but no tangible bodies. They were moving but making no noise. The Holy Spirit told me that they were the ones who are responsible for looking after the earth. Those images immediately fell down and worshiped the man who was standing in front of me. I didn't know where I was, but I knew that I came from Him and belonged to Him. I also fell down before Him, not daring to make any noise or raise my head.

Then I noticed we were surrounded by water. The water looked like a vast sea. As I was watching, the water started to fade away from us before my eyes. Something rose up from under our feet like the summit of a mountain. It supported my feet and His feet. Then it leveled out in all directions naturally. The place where we were became flat and it was completely dry. All the noise from the world disappeared at the moment. The air stopped moving; the wind stopped blowing. A total silence fell at once.

After a little while, I wanted to see what His face looked like. So I started to raise my head, but a strong light blinded my eyes causing a flood of tears. I could not open my eyes at all. Then I lifted my right arm in front of me to block that light so that my eyes would not be burned, but even my arm could not block that light. It was hurting me badly, and tears poured continuously from my eyes. I finally put my face down again in front of Him and dared not to move even an inch.

A moment later, I thought to myself again, *Who is He? What does He look like? I want to see His face.* So I put both arms in front of my eyes and raised my head once again. However, the strong light hurt me and I felt as if it could penetrate my arms. Tears flowed out of my eyes, but this time I could narrow my eyes into a very small slit and could peer out occasionally.

He was very tall and wearing a robe. Behind Him was an expansive, round, brilliant light shining with intense radiance. It was blindingly white like the dazzling white light from copper in a flame. I first thought that the light was the sun. "How can He stand inside of it?" I said to myself. At once, a voice came to me: "No, that is not the sun." That's right. I had never before seen such a strong brilliance. It was perhaps thousands of times stronger than the summer sun. It was unparalleled. He stood in front of that light, yet the light and He were together. They were inseparable.

28

I was only able to peer out occasionally. The great light hurt my eyes, and I was in tears the whole time. I blinked constantly and narrowed my eyes into very small slits so that I could continue. Finally, I could no longer stand the intense pain, and I gave up the idea of seeing His face. I put my face down in front of Him one more time.

The light came from behind His body and reflected His whole outline. Between that light and me, His figure formed a protective shadow so that the light didn't hit me directly but radiated to both sides of my body. In front of that white light, I trembled with great fear. Then I thought, *I am fortunate to have Him standing in front of me; I could not face the light or exist without His presence.*

He stood there quietly saying nothing. Then a pair of clear, beautiful, sharp, bright, piercing eyes appeared in front of me. I had never seen eyes as beautiful as this. In those eyes, there was tenderness with strictness, love with anger, and caring with blame, but what showed more than anything else was the expression of total affection. I was afraid of His eyes, because they had the ability to penetrate through everything. They seemed to see through all my joints and marrow and penetrate through my thoughts and mind. In front of Him, I felt even my soul was naked and nothing could be hidden.

Suddenly, He raised His right hand and drew a semicircle from His left shoulder to His right. I saw a beam of bright white light as brilliant as the light behind Him. It passed through the palm of His hand and moved along with His hand when He drew the semicircle. Immediately time turned back in this vision I was experiencing, and everything that had happened in my life including all the words that I had said, all the things that I had done, and all the thoughts that I had had, reappeared in front of me just like a movie. In this movie I first saw my young mother wearing a pigtail. After the man in front of me pointed to her womb, a spirit moved into it and her belly began to grow. He pointed in one direction and then market stalls appeared, one after another. He pointed again, and all kinds of foods were on display, each in its own stall. Then I saw my mother with her big belly going to the stalls to buy food. She ate, and I continued to grow in her womb until I was born.

From the moment my spirit moved into my mother's belly, the man's eyes never left me. My mother's womb was transparent to Him. It was clear to me that He had been intimately acquainted with my growth. When my mother was in labor, she was put in a small room, and several people busily tried to help. When I was born they all disappeared. I only saw the man standing in front of me next to my mother. I could feel He was smiling and His face was filled with love and kindness. He was waiting for me. When my naked and bloody body came out of my mother's womb, He delivered me and welcomed me into this world.

In this vision, my naked body wasn't in His arms, but suspended above them, turning clockwise rapidly in three hundred and sixty degree turns. While I was turning, I was growing up. I grew a lot after each rotation. Then, suddenly, my previous life appeared above my growing body at the same time. I watched my past be gradually revealed in shocking pictures. My mouth was gaping, and I was speechless.

Under His arm appeared a big white scroll. As my body was turning, the scroll unfolded by itself from left to right, and I saw many words written on it. I started to read the words on the scroll, and the more I read, the more I trembled with fear. These are the words I saw on the scroll:

From the time she was born she often cried with no reason at all to deceive others and gain their attention: the sin of lying. Pushed other children to the ground to get a chance to play on the swing: the sin of meanness. Fought with other kids with no mercy: the sin of bullying. Sought to be the center of attention: the sin of conceit. Quarreled and put others down: the sin of contention. Burst out in anger frequently: the sin of no self-control. Said bad words to others: the sin of cursing. Copied classmate's homework and deceived teachers and parents: the sin of cheating.

I could not stop and continued to read what was written on the scroll: *Didn't listen to parents' well-meaning teaching and chose to do forbidden things: the sin of rebellion. Hated parents' discipline: the sin of hostility. Caused parents sadness and tears thoughtlessly: the sin of disrespecting parents, a deadly sin. Ate neighbor's grapes without getting permission: the sin of stealing. Blamed her older sister for things that she had not done to avoid taking responsibility: the sin of framing others. Went to a fortune-teller: the sin of idol worship, a deadly sin. Sowed discord through gossip: the sin of slander.*

Resented mother in law who favored sister-in-law: the sin of jealousy. Harbored thoughts of retaliating and killing her ex-husband: the sin of murder, a deadly sin. Slept with a man who was already married: the sin of adultery, a deadly sin.

There were many more sins, and the words "deadly sin" was written after many of them. I read all the way through to the moment when I stood before Him. There were more words written on the scroll. I wanted to read them, but the words became fuzzy and unclear, as if a thin veneer covered over them. Then gradually all the words disappeared.

All of these sins in front of me, one after another, made me shake with fright and almost took my breath away. Those indeed were all words that I had said, deeds that I had done, and thoughts that I had thought. All the details were recorded precisely and accurately—not a single omission or mistake was made. It was all written on the scroll. I could not deny or argue with even one word written there.

I had always thought that I was really a good person. I thought I was beautiful and gentle, pure hearted and kind, smart and considerate, not perfect but almost faultless. I thought I was law abiding and had never hurt anyone, but that was just how it looked on the outside. However, the man in front me didn't just see the outside. I was naked in front of Him already. He saw what was inside of me: my soul, my thinking, my heart, and my mind. He was peeling me just like one peels an onion, layer by layer. He revealed to me who I was. I saw myself clearly and truly.

Deep inside of my soul, I was, in fact, a filthy, foul, dirty person who had never stopped being a sinner. I was through and through a sinner. I didn't deserve to have my life; I didn't deserve to live in this world. I was not worthy to appear before Him. I felt unbearably ashamed like an animal. How I wished there was a hole next to me in the ground, so I could burrow down under and cover my disgrace.

I said to Him, "I am a sinner. I am a sinner. I deserve to die. I deserve to die. I should have died many times long before now. Let me go ahead and die. Let me go ahead and die." I dared not look at Him. With my eyes closed I kept knocking my forehead on the ground requesting to die. I knew I deserved the death sentence. I also believed that the man in front of me would pronounce my death sentence and then assign someone to drag me away for execution.

With my face pressed to the ground, I was waiting to die — willing to die. I knew beyond a shadow of a doubt that I would be put to death. However, nothing happened. Everything was still, quiet, and peaceful. I didn't know what to do. I asked myself, "Why doesn't anyone come and drag me off? What's He waiting for?"

Chapter 4

LOVE IN HIS BLOOD, LIGHT THROUGH HIS HANDS

This tremendous vision continued, and suddenly, I heard a voice sounding from heaven above. "My child, you have come back at last. I have been waiting for you for so long." It was a voice of love, full of kindness and warmth, and full of tenderness and satisfaction. I had never heard a voice like that in the world before. It was vigorous and deep, broad and extensive. It was so attractive that everywhere echoed with its waves.

"Who else is here?" Just when I wanted to raise my head to see who was talking to me, I felt something splashing on my face. I opened my eyes and saw something red on the ground in front of me. It was blood, scarlet drops of blood. How could there be blood? Where did it come from? Before I could understand, another drop fell to the ground. It splashed all over, some onto my face, some onto

His robe. *Dee-da, dee-da, dee-da.* One drop, two drops, three drops fell to the ground. The sound from the blood drops could be heard clearly. They fell slowly at first and then more rapidly. After a while, a pool of blood formed on the ground and then gradually spread out.

I wiped the blood spots off my face with my right hand and raised my head. It was then that I saw Him. The brilliant bright light behind Him had disappeared. He became a real living man. He stood high above the ground a few steps away from me. There was a hole on the left side of His heart. Blood and water were pouring out from the hole, making a clear *gu-gu, gu-gu, gu-gu* sound. The blood fell to the ground to the sound of *dee-da, dee-da, dee-da.* Each time a drop reached the ground, my heart felt taut, as if a heavy hammer was pounding on my heart.

He stood there quietly and allowed the scarlet blood to pour out. I saw that He was in great pain. "Who was so cruel and merciless to pierce such a big hole in His heart?" I asked myself. Immediately, the Holy Spirit told me that His blood was shed for my sins, and His pain was caused by my faults. All of my sins broke His heart.

All the sins that had been recorded in the scroll had hurt Him and had been hurting Him always: my depravity, debauchery, and immorality; my ignorance, stubbornness, and rebellion; my bitterness, resentment, and anger. Every sin that I had committed was a painful torment for Him, like a sharp knife that injured Him deeply. Never for a moment had I stopped. It was I who had broken His heart, caused Him pain, and caused Him to bleed.

35

He didn't say anything but looked at me intently. What eyes they were! I had never seen such an expression, and I knew I would never forget it. They contained all human emotions: acceptance in the midst of sorrow, kindness in the midst of grief, hope in the midst of disappointment, and mercy in the midst of pain. Even though He appeared frail and crushed, in His gaze and behind every emotion, I saw deep love that was beyond description. The love in His gaze would be engraved into anyone's soul and never fade away. And all of that love was pouring out on me. I was shaken thoroughly and tears filled my eyes.

That's true love. Is that really for me? I thought and looked around. There was no one else.

"Yes, it's for you." The words came immediately into my mind.

"But how can this be, I have nothing with which to repay you," I said to Him in my spirit.

"You never had anything without me, but I still love you and never expected anything back from you. Take it. My love for you will never change." Love came to me with those words.

Having never experienced such an unconditional love, I could not hold my feelings back. I burst into tears. Through my tears, I poured out to Him years of suffering. All of them were from the deepest part of my soul, which I had never been able to mention to anyone else before.

I cried to Him, "But why do you love me? Who am I that you should care about me? I am nothing. My parents never favored me. I grew up feeling inferior. When I gave birth to my daughter, her father left us in the hospital. I am an abandoned woman with a broken heart. I am lonely and in pain. Diligently I had searched for true love, yet I found nothing. I am worse than dirt or dust. Nobody has ever paid any attention to me. I have no value, no job, no money, and no home since the divorce. I am so tired, with no place to go and nothing to rely on. The only thing I have is my daughter, but I have to be separated from her. I do not want to live like this, but I have no choice, I was forced into it. The way I am living is without dignity or courage or hope or a future. I have nothing. Why do you love me?" I wept loudly.

He responded to me, "I genuinely love you. I have never moved my eyes away from you. I watched all your sufferings and I know you are in pain, yet my heart has more pain than yours because I have always loved you."

I wept even louder, "Had I known true love is in you, I would never have gone out searching for it, and I would never have made so many mistakes. But it's too late now. I am a sinner. I only deserve to perish. Everything has already been written in that scroll. I have to pay the price for what I have done wrong. A woman like me is even beyond knowing shame. I am foul and filthy. How could I deserve your love? No, I don't deserve it." I shook my head.

Before I had even finished thinking, He answered me in my spirit. "I tried very hard to tell you how much that I love you, but you refused me, and never gave me a chance to enter into your heart."

He wasn't trying to blame me. I knew what He said was true, and I felt foolish and regretful.

However, waves of love continued to come over me. His words continued, "It's never too late. Your past is not important to me. The only important thing is that you are the one I love. No matter what your background is, how poor and broken you are, how worthless you feel, how deep you have sinned, or whether you knew me or not, I still love you and will never abandon you. My love has never changed and it never will." Then images of sky, mountains, and seas appeared before me followed by more words: "Look at them. My love is higher than the sky, larger than the mountains, deeper than the sea. My love is boundless and beyond what you can imagine." Then He was silent. I looked into His eyes and at His bleeding heart, and I instantly knew He meant every word.

I wept bitterly. Then my past life flashed before my eyes again. I saw Him in my daily life. When I cried, He held me in His arms and comforted me. When I was hungry and thirsty, He fed me with milk, rice, and meat, and made me satisfied. When I was cold, He put a warm winter cotton-padded jacket on me with a floral design. When I fell down, He lifted me up, knocked the dust off of my clothes softly and checked if I had any scratches. He held me by my hands and helped me try again. When I wanted to travel, He held my luggage behind me and directed me to the road. When I was sick and weak, He came to my bedside and gave me strength. When I was lonely, He stood by the window and was there to keep me company. When

I was sad, He gently wiped my tears away. When I was rebellious, He disciplined me. Always the pain in His heart was greater than the pain I felt because He wanted to bring me, the prodigal child, back to Him. When I started to make changes for the better, He then provided me with things that I had really longed for.

Countless moments of love and grace passed before my eyes. I saw that I was so valuable in His eyes, worthy of being cherished, and deserving of His earnest love and care. Because of love, He was willing to take all my sins upon Himself, to bear sorrows for me, to endure pain alone in silence, and to let His blood flow. Because of love, He chose to wait in pain so that His ignorant and tired child would return home. Because of love, He tolerated and forgave me without saying a condemning word to me.

My soul was deeply touched. I also had a feeling of great sorrow, as if a sharp knife was cutting my heart. I could hardly bear it. I knew my sorrow was from watching His heart bleed for my sins. The pain that I felt was only a tiny bit of what He was carrying. One cannot imagine how much His pain was.

Then my conscience told me immediately: *My sins alone badly hurt Him and deeply broke His heart. There are so many people in this world. Everyone has sinned against Him. How badly must He hurt? How deeply is His heart broken? Each time I committed a sin, it was like a sharp knife piercing His heart causing Him to shed blood. If everyone in the world committed just one sin, how many sharp knives would pierce His heart? How much and how long would He shed His blood? If things continued like this, His blood would completely drain out.*

My heart ached greatly, and I yelled to Him anxiously and loudly, "Stop bleeding. Stop bleeding. Your blood will be drained." Yet He didn't move. He was willing to give up His life for me. I wished I could wrap His injury or stop His bleeding, but I could not reach Him. I started to wail at the top of my voice. I had never cried with such a broken heart. Tears flowed down like rivers and streams. In fact, it wasn't crying but a kind of emotional explosion. I felt deep regret for all the sins that I had committed. It was a most sincere repentance from my heart of hearts.

At that moment, I hated myself. I had never felt like that ever before. Even the ox knows his master, and the donkey his owner's manger, but I didn't know the One who gave me life and loved me so deeply. As I was crying, a veil lifted from my heart. I started to blame myself for all the things that I had done wrong. He gave me a conscience to know Him. However, my conscience had run away from Him after I had enough to eat and drink. I was like an ignorant horse, stubborn and unruly, and I didn't even think to reflect back on who had met my daily needs. Neither did I feel grateful nor did I ask myself, "Who is giving all this to me?" I took the fullness that He gave to me for granted and rejected His love with ignorance and coldness. I had turned my back on Him and kept committing sins. I hurt Him by stabbing His heart with the "knife of sin." I caused Him to suffer and bleed for me until He was at the point of death. Was this what I gave in return to the man who loved me with all of His heart? How could I treat Him like this?

I could not forgive myself. How could I? I was such an ungrateful person! I was sinful and should die, but even my death was not sufficient for such sins. I was incredibly wrong. If I could start all over again, I would never sin against Him or hurt Him anymore. It was too late. I could neither change the past nor turn back time. I felt so guilty that I dared not face Him or ask His forgiveness. I knew I didn't deserve it. I could only kneel in front of Him like a child who makes so many mistakes kneels before her father who loves her. I wouldn't hide my crying because of the guilt in my heart.

Suddenly, I felt someone embrace me tightly. I opened my eyes and saw two arms of soft golden light surrounding me firmly. They made me feel so complete and I knew I could rely on them. I could not believe my eyes. I looked from the left to the right and then from the right to the left. I touched the arms with my hands. Immediately, an intense love like warm currents ran through my whole body. The Love from this world can only be felt, but the love from Him could be touched. His love wiped away my guilt and tears. Instantly, I was comforted. An immeasurable contentment and peace came upon me all at once. It was a peace that this world can't possibly give.

When I raised my head and looked again, He was back in front of the bright light, the way He had been when I first saw Him. He was a shining light with boundless radiance. This great light that surrounded Him hurt my eyes again. I was in tears and could only peer out occasionally to look at Him. I saw Him raise His right hand and draw a semicircle from His left shoulder to His right. I saw a beam of bright white light as brilliant as the light behind Him when He drew the semicircle. It passed through the palm of His hand. This was the second time I saw the beam of light. It was exactly like the light I had seen earlier. Then a man's voice, the same voice that I had heard before, came from heaven above, "Go, help her." The voice was majestic and awesome, vast and open, deep and profound. The voice had no sense of haste. It was like thunder rumbling in all directions with great power and absolute authority. Then everywhere surrounded by His silence and this great vision began to disappear.

Chapter 5

THERE IS A GOD WHO
JUDGES THE EARTH

After the vision receded from my consciousness, I opened my eyes and could not believe I was still alive floating on the surface of the sea. I thought that I had died and I was in a different place. In front of me was a young fellow. He said to me, "Do not be afraid. Put your hands on my shoulders. I will take you out of the water." He put his right hand on his left shoulder and said to me, "Do this. Just ride on my shoulders very lightly." Then he moved his hand to his neck and said, "Do not do this. If you hold my neck tightly, I will not be able to breathe, and we will both sink." I understood immediately that the One from above whom I had just seen had sent him to me. So I put my hands on his shoulders, closed my eyes, and let him take me.

This young man took me back to the shore and held me up as we walked back to the beach. I shivered and felt something like an electric current passing through my body. It made me stagger. I wanted to tell him that I couldn't walk and needed to lie down for a rest, but I was exhausted. I didn't even have strength to keep my eyes open let alone talk. I signaled to him with my hands, and then my whole body started to collapse.

"No, you cannot lie here. When the waves come, you will be taken away," the young fellow said to me. He half dragged and half supported me further up the beach to where the waves could not reach me and he thought I was safe. I lay down at once and went into a deep sleep. I don't know how long I slept.

After I woke up, I found Bert on the beach. He was watching the sea. When he saw me, he asked me curiously, "Where did you go? You have been gone for so long. I could not find you anywhere."

I said to him, "A bi-bi-big wa-wa-wave" I wanted to tell him that I had seen a big wave and nearly drowned, but I found I had a stuttering problem and could not express myself. As soon as I opened my mouth to speak about my experience, I trembled all over. My lips shivered nonstop, and my tongue became stiff. At last, Bert understood me. He looked at me with confusion, shook his head, and said, "No, I have been watching the sea. It was very calm." He thought I was joking so he didn't take my remarks seriously.

I said to him, "Ba-ba-back to-to-to the ro-ro-room." I wanted to tell him that we should go back to the hotel room that I would tell him what happened, but I could not explain any more because that same electric current went through my body again, making me tremble.

"But it's too early to go back. Let's stay a little longer." Bert looked at me with some perplexity.

Ignoring him, I bent down and started to fold my bath towel. Bert probably noticed my face did not look normal, so he got up and started to walk with me to the hotel. On the way back, I walked like a drunkard. He tried to hold on to me but I threw off his hands. While I was doing so, I looked around and felt many eyes were staring at me from everywhere. I understood then that my whereabouts were not a secret. The man from above was watching me. He knew everything about me.

I was afraid to meet anyone. The minute we walked into the elevator, someone else got in as well. I slowly moved my body to a corner, hoping that no one would take any notice of me. I felt so ashamed and no words could describe my humiliation.

Back in the hotel room, I sat in front of the makeup mirror. In the mirror my face looked pale and lifeless. My eyes were filled with horror. My body and heart were still trembling. I was still shocked by what I had gone through in the sea. Bert didn't understand what had happened. Not long before, I had walked out of the room lively and with lots of spirit, but now I had become totally dull as if I were dead.

Bert walked to me from the other side of the room and tried to hug and comfort me, but I was so frightened that I didn't want him to touch me. I knew there was a third party with us in the room: the man from above who had appeared to me in the sea. Nothing about me could be hidden from His eyes. He was recording my thoughts and my deeds. Everything I did would be written down in that open scroll, and not a single word would be missing. That made me very scared.

The man who I had seen in my vision appeared before my eyes. His figure was frail and weak, and His eyes were deep and filled with love. He looked at me intently. I felt restless and uneasy. I was afraid to see Him, but He appeared before me no matter where I was.

I had no way of avoiding His image. When I sat in front of the mirror, He stood in the mirror. When I closed my eyes, He was in front of me. When I buried my face into my hands, He was in my palms. When I covered my face with the sheet, He appeared under the sheet. When I went into the washroom, closed the door, and turned off the lights, He stood by the door. When I walked out of the room onto the balcony, He was already waiting for me there. When I closed all the windows, He stood by the window. I just could not get away from His spirit and face. He was with me. We were inseparable.

I tossed and turned all night, unable to calm down or sleep. My heart was churning like boiling water. I was so tired that I didn't want to recall what I had gone through that afternoon in the ocean, but the vision came back to my mind again and again, and every single detail was clear. I shook my head very hard and thought to myself, *No, no, no, I don't want to see this again. I don't want to see this again.* However, I could not control my thoughts. My vision repeated itself in my mind incessantly. That night was the longest, hardest, and most unforgettable night of my life.

That night many questions flooded my mind. Who was He—the man I saw in my vision? What kind of light was that and why had I never seen such a light in this world? Why couldn't I stand in front of that light? How could the light pass through the palm of His hand? Why did He give me a second chance to live instead of sending me off to die? How could He know everything about me, but I knew nothing about Him? Why was He everywhere with me, but I had never seen Him before? Why did He appear to me, and why didn't He pull me up from the sea directly but instead send that young fellow to save me?

I wanted to stop asking myself questions, but I could not stop my mind. Questions came to me continuously: Where was I and what kind of place was that? Wasn't the devil crushing my throat? Where did the devil's hands go? How did the man in my vision know my language? How could He react so fast—even faster than the wind when I asked for help? How could I see Him when I closed my eyes, but those people on the beach could not when they had their eyes wide open? How? How? How? Why? Why? Why?

Questions filled my mind. I wanted to know the answers. I had to find the answers. I thought, *Obviously, I died once today, but how did I come back to life? What were the last words I spoke before my death? How did the man come to me from above?*

I started to recall the scene and analyze it carefully. The devil had ridden on the top of the wave and had come toward me. He had roared, "I am going to destroy you today!" I had stretched out my arms to heaven with my hands open. Two words had come out of my mouth: "My God!" Then I had closed my eyes and waited to die. I stopped myself and thought: *Wait a minute. I am an atheist. I have never believed in God's existence before, nor have I had any God in my heart. I would never have asked God for help, so how could the words "My God" have come out of my mouth? That must not have been me, but who else could it have been since I was there alone?*

I didn't understand how this had happened. Nevertheless, those two words had come out of my own mouth. After calling out, heaven had opened and the clouds had hovered above. "The Holy Spirit!" I had exclaimed. Again I stopped myself and thought: *Wait a minute. I have never heard anything about the Holy Spirit before nor have I ever seen Him. How could these words have come out of my mouth?* I didn't understand this either. In any event, the Holy Spirit had come down, folded His wings, turned around, and a pillar of cloud had become a human being. The image of a man had stood in front of me.

Yes, indeed, "My God" had been the last two words out of my mouth before my death, and then He had appeared. I continued to think: *Does God really exist? Could He be the One? If He wasn't God but someone else, and if I didn't call upon Him, why did He show up when I called upon the name of God in my danger? What was He doing there? That means the man I saw could only be God, the one who answered my call. But shouldn't God be very extraordinary? Why was He the same as me, and why did He take a human image?* I had no answer to these questions.

I only knew He had appeared from heaven when I had called His name and that I had seen what I had seen: light, brilliant light, and radiance. Light had gone through the palm of His hand. He had drawn the semicircle, and my whole life reappeared. I had seen my sins, many deadly sins. I had admitted to them all and asked for death. I had heard a voice sound from above, "My child, you have come back at last. I have been waiting for you for so long!" Then I had seen His blood, His body, and His eyes. Another semicircle was drawn, and then the light had gone through the palm of His hand again. A voice from heaven had sounded again, "Go, help her." When everything had disappeared, I had opened my eyes and had seen the young fellow who had saved my life.

After considering the details of this vision, I became even more frightened than when I had faced death earlier. I thought to myself, *There is a God who judges the earth, but I didn't know this. What kind of place is this? It's the temple of God, and the gate of heaven. Here, I met God face to face. Here, I saw the One who gave me life and a soul. Here, I heard His voice, which was like waves and thunder. Here, He sent someone to save me. None of this was a dream or a hallucination. What I saw and how I felt were real. I could not possibly have made it up.*

At midnight that night, my heart was still trembling, my legs were still shaking, and my body was still shivering. I could not sleep. I went to the balcony with all of these questions in my mind. The balcony faced the sea, and the night sky was overcast without any signs of life. The pounding of the crashing waves from the sea was like a giant hammer striking against my heart, making me tremble even more. Holding the rail of the balcony and facing the night sky, I stared out as in a daze.

When the hot air blew over my cheeks and the palm trees swayed with the hot air, I saw the man in my vision again. He was standing under the night sky not far away from me. I could see His image but not His face. Suddenly, countless eyes appeared around Him, the scene made me feel scared. He pointed above with His right hand and immediately a voice spoke inside of me, "Who placed the stars in the night sky? If you were to ask the stars, each one of them would know the answer."

Raising my head, I looked at the sky. Each star seemed to be nodding to me, indicating that they did know the answer. Suddenly, as I was watching the stars, they became hundreds and thousands of pairs of eyes, staring down at me. Some of the stars seemed to ridicule me that I didn't understand, and others seemed to sympathize with my fright. I felt so stupid. Even the stars knew the truth, so why didn't I? Why had no one ever told me? Why had everybody lied to me by saying that there was no God of creation? Where were the people who could speak the truth? These questions led me to reflect on my past life and those who had educated me.

Chapter 6

THE TRUE GOD IS
ALIVE, NOT DEAD

I remembered teachers in school instructing us that the human race had evolved from monkeys and that after many years of evolution, monkeys had become human beings. My parents had told me that after bad things happen to people, they become disappointed and feel empty with nothing to rely on, so they fabricate the idea of a something out of nothing and give that nothing the name God. My neighbors, classmates, and friends all told me that there was no God. God was a figment of people's imaginations. But God was there with me in the sea. My mind was completely clear when I went into the sea till the last minute of my life. Indeed, I saw Him. He wasn't a figment of my imagination, and this God saved me. How could I deny this fact?

I came to realize that people were lying. No one, not even a single person, was telling me the truth. I had grown up in an environment of deceit. I had been cheated for twenty-seven years. How long would people continue to lie? If I hadn't seen Him with my very own eyes and experienced Him myself, I would still be in darkness. How terrible!

I started to blame everyone that I knew for cheating me and treating me like a complete idiot. I could no longer trust them or believe their theory about God, especially my parents. I had totally trusted and depended on them since I was born. How could they also lie to me and not tell me the truth about God's existence? How could they treat me like that?

The more I thought about it, the more upset I became. The most ridiculous thing was that I had believed their words without thinking for a moment about it myself. I hadn't spent even a few minutes thinking about whether their words were true or not. If there isn't a God, then where do the flowers, grass, and trees come from? Where do the mountains, streams, and rivers come from? Where do the moon, sun, and stars come from? Where do the snow, mist, high winds, and heavy rain come from? When I asked my teachers these questions, they answered that those things were just naturally there. I was told not to ask about these kinds of questions. I obeyed. In my school at that time, I would have been considered a bad student if I had asked more questions. I would have been treated as a disrupter of the class. I would have been punished and made to stand outside the classroom. When I asked my parents, they told me that whatever the teacher said was the right answer. My parents also told me not to ask any more questions. They told me to be a good student.

That's why I had never asked more. But why hadn't I seen and realized that there is a God even without the assistance of my teachers, parents, and friends? Why hadn't I recognized the existence of God for so many years? Did I really not know? Or did I not want to know? Or did I fear to know? I could not answer these questions.

At this moment, I was coming to a new realization. It was God who allowed me to be born into a world full of life. He prepared the sun to warm me, and provided the air for me to breathe. He covered the mountains with grass, placed flowers in front of me, and made trees to bear fruit. He ordered streams to tumble through mountains and exhorted birds to sing in the branches. He made the breeze kiss my cheeks and white clouds to wander in the blue sky. He filled the world with life and made that life multiply. Every day He tried to show me something of His creation, to tell me of His existence, to demonstrate His true love, and to assert that He was the Master of life. Every day He tried to teach me that He was the source of all things and the origin of life. He had given me so many opportunities to know Him.

However, I couldn't see His creation, even though I had eyes. I couldn't hear His words, even though I had ears. I refused the truth, even though I had a heart. I didn't think and persisted in my old ways, even though I had a brain. There were three hundred and sixty-five days in a year, and I had lived for twenty-seven years. He had given me more than nine thousand days to see and more than two hundred thousand hours to hear. I had my eyes open every day, yet I still hadn't recognized His presence all around me in my life. I had ears to listen all that time, yet I still hadn't heard His voice. If I wasn't blind or deaf, then what was I? I was totally stupid. I was amazed at my own stupidity.

Then I thought of the statues that my grandmother worshipped at home. To my astonishment, the God I saw wasn't like the statues that she had worshiped. He wasn't the Buddha with a huge belly and big smile, nor was He the Goddess of Mercy sitting on the lotus throne with thousands of hands sticking out of her. My grandmother was a devout Buddhist. Several times a year, she would spend her hard-earned money to buy groceries, and then would go to a certain place with the delicious food that she had prepared to worship the Goddess of Mercy. This practice was to ward off any family disaster. At her home, she would burn incense to the Goddess of Mercy placed on a high stand in order to keep the household safe. I thought of my mother too. In my hometown my mother used to take me to the top of the hill to bow down to the idols made of stones or earth; thus, we would obtain peace, wealth, and health.

But when I was in danger and begging for my life, why didn't the Buddha and the Goddess of Mercy that my ancestors worshiped appear? Didn't they have eyes and ears, hands and feet on their bodies? Didn't people worship them in their homes and temples?

Didn't people burn incense and bow down to them daily? Why didn't these "gods" have any feelings of mercy for me when I was in that desperate situation? Why didn't they move even though they had bodies? Why couldn't they hear my cry even though they had ears? Why couldn't they see my misery even though they had eyes? Why couldn't they reach out to me even though they had hands? Why couldn't they come to my side even though they had feet?

I suddenly understood. They were all false gods, made and painted by human hands. They were all dead, lifeless, loveless, and spiritless. How could statues move around when someone's hands had made them? How could they save me when they were dead? How could they love me when they had no love? How could they give me life when they had no life? How could they sense any feelings for me when they had no spirit? What is true cannot become false, and what is false can never become true. They were not the true God. The only true God was the One I saw.

This true God came from above the dense clouds. He had wings like a great bird, which protected me. He had a body in the image of a human being just like me. He had love that was touchable. He had eyes that could see through my heart and mind. His eyes could speak. They told me how much He loved me, and they spoke with strong emotion. They were strict but filled with kindness, affection and mercy. He had ears that could hear my cry. He had arms that could reach out, hug me, and make me feel how much I could rely on him. He had hands that drew a semicircle in which I could see all my past sins. He had palms through which a stream of light passed. He had feet that could stand inside that bright light, and behind Him was the brilliant, boundless radiance. He had a mouth through which to speak, and He had a voice through which He made sound. He called me His child. He said He had been waiting for me for so long, and He summoned that young fellow to come and save my life. He had a wounded heart with a hole in it from which blood poured out, and the blood was shed for me. The blood that splashed onto His robe was proof of His life.

What I saw with my own eyes changed my belief. The true God exists, not the Buddha, not the Goddess of Mercy, and not any statues! The true God is alive, not dead. He is the living God. All of a sudden, I asked myself, "Why do nearly all Chinese people not believe in this real and living God? Why do so many of them worship the Buddha and the Goddess of Mercy statues? Who told them to do so? How did this mistake start and where did it come from?"

I started to think carefully about the reason for my family's misconception of God. My grandparents had guided my parents. If my grandparents were wrong, of course my parents would be wrong. My grandparents had been taught by their forefathers. If their forefathers hadn't known the truth, of course they would have taught their children that these false deities were the true god and goddess. This kind of teaching from generation to generation confused the real truth. When it came down to me, the worship of the Buddha or the

Goddess of Mercy was already the traditional culture and had been so for thousands of years. This was indeed an error with deep roots.

I came to the conclusion that people like my ancestors, parents, teachers, friends, and neighbors are blind if they don't know the true God. I had been led by the blind since my birth. How silly that was! If a blind person leads another blind person to cross a single log bridge with no railing, how can they know where they are if they both fall into a dark gully below? If a blind person treats another blind person's eye disease, how can they expect to see light when they are both still groping in the dark? If a blind person guides another blind person home, how can they experience the true happiness of coming home if they're both lost and go through the wrong door? No wonder I could not see God. All Chinese people have been deceived, and I felt I was the only one who knew the real truth. I decided I would expose the hoax of false gods and tell the truth to everyone when I got back to Chengdu. This thought made me feel much better.

Then I started to think about the fact that there was no one around me who admitted to God's existence, so how could I prove that I saw God? Then I thought, *Tomorrow I will find the young fellow who pulled me out of the water. I will have dinner with him to thank him for saving my life. I will ask him where he had seen me, how he had heard my cry when the two men near me could not, and from where had he come.* I had heard God saying, "Go, help her." Clearly, that hadn't been said to me. Had it been said to him? Had he also heard

God speaking? Had he been sent just for me? If so, then that would prove that the God I saw was real.

I walked back into the room, hoping to tell Bert what I thought. However, my tears came pouring out even before I opened my mouth. I could hardly complete a sentence. I shook my head and motioned to Bert to give me a piece of paper and a pencil. Then I wrote down a few words with a trembling hand: Young fellow saved me, dinner, thank him. Bert didn't get all the details, but somehow he understood that an extraordinary thing must have happened, and he agreed to have dinner with that young man.

There were two single beds in the room. I lay on one of them and Bert on the other. I dared not sleep with him after the vision I saw in the ocean. This was the only way that I could feel a little bit of peace. Nevertheless, my heart wasn't the same. I continued to reflect through the night. *Will that young fellow still be there tomorrow? Will I be able to find him? Will he accept my invitation? How can I ask him about the God that I had never heard anyone talk about before? What is he going to say to me?*

I didn't know. Everything was a mystery, and the secret wouldn't be uncovered until the next day. That was a restless night. I kept asking myself why the night was so long. Why hadn't the dawn come yet? Why hadn't the sun risen?

NOTHING IS A COINCIDENCE

I managed to make it to dawn. When the sun finally shone into the hotel room, I found that I could not open my eyes. My eyes felt burning, and tears kept running out of them. In order to open my eyes, I had to wear a pair of sunglasses even inside the hotel room. I didn't go out for breakfast. Instead, I asked Bert to bring it back to me. After the breakfast, it was still too early, and I dared not go into the ocean, so I stayed by the hotel swimming pool to pass the time. I waited impatiently until about 9:30 a.m. and then went to the Da Dong Hai Beach with Bert. Very few people were there, and I didn't see the young fellow who saved me the day before.

"Perhaps it's too early for him to come. Let's wait for a bit and hope he will come," said Bert. He put down the bath towel on the beach, and I sat on it. He invited me to go into the water with him, but I dared not. I was so frightened of the sea after what had happened the previous afternoon. I was afraid to see the ocean and hear the sound it made. I stayed far away from the water, I was afraid of being washed away by the waves. Bert went in by himself. Quietly, I sat there alone.

But my heart wasn't quiet. I saw the place where I had stood the day before. The sea was shallow with an extremely calm surface. The soft and gentle beach extended toward the water beneath, and seagulls sometimes flew under the blue sky and rested on the beach. Several naked boys were frolicking in the shallow water. What a peaceful picture. I thought back to the day before. I could not stop thinking what a safe area it was. Even the parents allowed their children to play there freely. How could two hands hide there and drag me down without any warning?

What I had experienced the previous afternoon came back to me. It was like a video tape playing repeatedly in my mind. I could not stop it. I lost count of how many times I went through it. I continued thinking. *It was just yesterday that I almost lost my life. I almost lost the opportunity to see this beautiful scenery. I almost lost hearing the sounds of these waves. I almost lost feeling the hot air blowing on my face. If God hadn't sent someone to save me, then I would no longer be alive. I would have disappeared forever from this world, and no one would even know where I was except me.* I shivered. How short my life is. It's not controlled by me, but by God. How ignorant I used to be, and how wrong my view of life was. Facing the ocean, I felt smaller than ever.

After some time, the fellow who had saved me finally appeared. He was dressed in a blue T-shirt and a pair of shorts. He sat down not far from me. I was afraid he would disappear from my sight if I didn't immediately say something, so I hurried over to him. I hadn't seen him clearly until that moment. He was a very shy fellow, perhaps twenty five to thirty years old. He had dark brown skin. He was thin but energetic. I could sense his simple, honest, and smart character from his smile.

I greeted him, "Hello."

"Hello." He looked at me with a smile.

"Thank you. You saved me yesterday." I looked at him. He also looked at me and smiled, but he didn't reply.

"Thank you. You saved me yesterday," I repeated, but he still had no response, as if he didn't understand what I was saying. That was very strange. Didn't he know that I was talking to him?

Someone next to him smiled at me and said something to him. He then nodded his head, "Oh." He then shook his head and said something that I didn't understand. The person next to him said to me, "He said, 'My pleasure, my pleasure.' He said that he's sorry. He is a native of this island with hardly any education and can't speak Mandarin fluently."

I responded, "I see." Then I thought to myself, *When he came to me yesterday he said to me, do not be afraid. Put your hand on my shoulder. I will take you out of the water. Every single word was clear.*

Nevertheless, I didn't ask him any questions about this even though I didn't understand what was going on.

I said to the stranger next to him, "Please tell him that I want to invite him for dinner tonight to thank him for saving my life yesterday. Ask him whether he can come or not."

The stranger interpreted my words to the young fellow in their local language and then said, "He said, 'Thanks for inviting me, but it's not necessary. It was my pleasure to help you.'"

I insisted, and he finally agreed to come but with a requirement, which was to bring his best friend, an educated man who spoke Mandarin and could be an interpreter. I agreed, "Okay, that's settled. Six o'clock this evening at the hotel where I am staying." I showed him the direction of my hotel. He nodded.

They came on time at 6:00 p.m. We had a very pleasant talk during dinner, although we started with insignificant chatter. When the dinner was almost done, I asked the young fellow only one question. "Where were you when I was in danger? How did you see me?" I didn't mention a single word of how God had appeared to me. If he told me it was God who told him to come for me, then what I had experienced yesterday wasn't a dream or hallucination. It would mean that the God I met was true and authentic.

He said to me through his best friend, "In fact, I didn't see you at all. I was in my little cottage and was in the middle of my shower, and my bare body was covered in soap bubbles. Suddenly, I heard someone say, 'Go, help her.' I grabbed some shorts, yanked them on and then rushed outside at once. I asked some workers outside of my little cottage, "Who? Where?" They didn't understand what I was talking about. I asked them again, "Who needs help? And where?" They pointed to where you were. I looked in that direction but could hardly see you. I could just see the top of your head bobbing up and down with the waves. Then I ran toward you at top speed. I went into the water and swam to you as fast as I could, and then I pulled you out of the water."

I could not believe my ears after listening to what he said. I lowered my head and didn't want to eat any more. After being silent for a while, I asked the young fellow, "Did the workmen outside of your little cottage say to you, 'Go, help her?'"

"No, they didn't say that, and they didn't hear who was speaking to me. But someone did speak that to me, and I heard it. That's why I rushed out of my cottage," he said.

"How did they know that I was in danger?" I asked him.

"Perhaps they saw both of your hands up and knew you could not stay afloat any longer. They watch the sea every day and have experience." He replied.

"Are you here for a vacation?" I asked him.

"No, I am not. I live by the sea," he answered.

"You must be a good swimmer. It requires a very strong body to run from your cottage to the water and then swim to me." I admired his physical strength.

"I used to be a lifeguard," he said. "Maybe you do not know that Sanya used to be a hot destination for many real-estate investors. However, there are less and less people who come to this island due to a change in government policies. I lost my job. I have nothing to do now, so I just swim around in the ocean every day. I had already swum several times yesterday. My body was very sticky, and I felt uncomfortable, so I went back to my little cottage to take a shower. That's why I was in the middle of the shower with nothing on when you were in danger," he said with an embarrassed smile.

"Where is your cottage? Can you please take me there to have a look?" I wanted to know how far away he was from me at that time.

"No, please do not come. My place is too poor. It's just a thatched shack, old and broken down with nothing in it. I would feel embarrassed showing it to you. You'd better not come," he said shyly looking at Bert at the same time. According to our humble culture, we Chinese people never want to show our homes to foreigners if it's shabby. Since he firmly turned me down I couldn't pursue it any further.

On the way back to the hotel room, I kept thinking that this young fellow had really heard the voice of God. He really had been sent just for me. The scene flashed back in my mind again and again. I remembered God had said, "Go, help her!" When I opened my eyes, He was the one I saw. Was this a coincidence? How could it be? No, it was not, absolutely not! It was impossible that it was a coincidence. Through the mouth of this young fellow, I once again confirmed that what I had experienced the day before was not a dream, an illusion, or my imagination. It was God Himself who had come and rescued me.

This is a mighty and powerful God. He had known what was going to happen before I even reached this destination. He had prepared not only one pair of eyes but also multiple pairs of eyes to watch over me from a distance. He had prepared this young fellow, not an ordinary man, but a well-qualified and professional lifeguard. Those strangers had been placed in key spots and were ready for me when I cried out for help. What an amazing arrangement! How could it be a coincidence?

Not only that, the most important thing was that God Himself was waiting for me. He had revealed Himself and had let me see His bleeding, experience His pure love, and understand His mercy and forgiveness so that I could recognize Him and come back to Him. I came to know that from the time I was born, all the pain that I had experienced was for this moment. No wonder I had been longing for the sea. No wonder that when I had first seen the ocean, I felt it was my home. The sea led me to God.

At this point I realized that this was not due to the ocean but to God whom I met in my vision. He wanted to meet me there. It turned out that nothing was a coincidence. There never had been any coincidences. Everything had been arranged beforehand by the will of God. He had waited for me to be in Sanya, to learn His mighty power, to recognize His unconditional love, to understand His grace and mercy, and to find the way to heaven. He had been giving me the chance to confess, to come back to His arms, and to be united with Him, but I knew nothing about His good will before my journey to Sanya.

Before this trip I was an atheist. I lived in sin and I had come to the ocean—the heaven of my dreams—yet I didn't know that what I had waited for would lead me to my death. However, when I saw God's blood and was forgiven by Him, I gained a new life from my death. Oh, what an amazing God He is! He was declaring to me that death is not the end, the soul has a place to go, heaven is not in this world, life can be eternal, and eternal life is in Him.

Chapter 8

HE WOKE UP MY SOUL

*B*ack at the hotel room, I couldn't sleep for the second night. Closing my eyes, I saw God standing in front of me. He engaged my mind completely with His image, His voice, His movements, His brilliant light, His blood, His love, His palm and the light passing through His palm. That night God woke up my soul. I suddenly understood the truth that I had never even thought of before. I had no exposure to Christian teaching or the Bible. Nevertheless, I came to believe in God and these were some of my conclusions based on my vision.

First, I became profoundly aware that there really is a God of creation in the universe. God is Spirit and comes from above. He is greater than anything and everything. He can change Himself and take the image of a human being. A brilliant and dazzling light is with Him wherever He is. He is the Creator who gave me life and who gives life to all. He brought me out of my mother's womb. From birth, I was cast upon Him. From my mother's womb He has been my God even though I did not know Him.

Second, I realized that heaven and hell really exist, as do angels and devils, and the judgment after death. Human beings are a combination of flesh and soul, and the flesh is dead without the soul. Flesh can only stay on earth after death, and the soul will be judged by what is written in the scroll. The soul will be taken to heaven or hell on the basis of what a person has done or thought while he or she lived in the world. If a person does not know the real God, then his or her life is controlled by the devil. The result of this is when death comes, he or she will surely be taken to hell.

Another conclusion I came to was that life is a gift granted to my body by God. If He says, "Live," then I have life. If He says, "Die," then I have no breath. If at the ocean He had said, "Go to hell," then I couldn't have lived. It's not my choice whether I live or not. It was God who hid His face from my sin and who gave me the chance to live. It's His word that kept me alive. I am not the center of life, but God is. He is in control of my future. He is the Sovereign Master of life.

I concluded that God knows me, cares for me, draws near to me, and redeems me. He came down from His exalted throne above, to save an impure person like me, someone who was not even worth the dust or dirt on the ground. God could see my misery, and He heard my cry. He is a humble God, and He protected me at all times without resting. He knew my situation and came to me at once without any hesitation. If He had been just a little bit late, the devil would have taken me away. The Lord reacts with lightning speed, as soon as I closed my eyes, He appeared to me. He is the God that responds to our cries.

I realized that I was an absolute sinner and was intolerably filthy. I was born and had grown up in sin. Ever since my birth, I had been estranged from God. I had gone astray and had told lies. I did not deserve to be alive. It was God's grace and mercy, His slowness to wrath, and His abounding goodness and faithfulness, which forgave my sins and offenses and enabled me to live. He is the God who is full of mercy. I have never been alone. God's Spirit has been with me. The darkness could never be too dark for Him to see me. In His eyes the night is as bright as the day. Wherever I am, He is there. His eyes have never departed from me. He is the God who is present everywhere at the same time and at all times.

Based on this vision and what I learned about God, I decided that anyone who cannot see God is blind. Anyone who cannot hear God is deaf. Those people on the beach had their eyes open but didn't see His existence. They had their ears open but didn't hear His voice. That's why they were all blind and deaf. I was one of them, but I'm not anymore. God opened my eyes so I can see Him. He opened my ears so I can hear His voice. He opened my heart and woke up my soul, and I accepted Him. He is the God who makes the blind see and the deaf hear.

To my surprise I learned that there are no secrets in the world, and there is nothing that God doesn't know. He knew everything I had ever done and showed it all to me. He saw through my mind, thoughts, bone marrow, and soul. He set all my sins before Him, all my secret sins in the light of His face, and I could not hide any of my sins from Him. There are billions of people in the world. He didn't place others' transgressions upon me. He was accurate and made no mistake at all. Whatever I could remember, He remembered. Whenever I wasn't clear, He was clear. Whatever I had forgotten, He knew well. Nothing escaped His eyes.

I became conscious of the fact that life indeed is very short. My whole life is but a blink in the eyes of God, and then it's over. I cannot take anything with me when I die, such as position, authority, honor, money, jewels, or appliances. I came into this world with empty hands, and I will leave this world with empty hands. I am only a stranger on earth. I am just a traveler in this world.

Thankfully, I learned as well that nothing is a coincidence. There have never been coincidences. God plans and prepares for things way ahead of time. He has prepared Himself for us, and He is waiting for the right time to come so everything will happen in His way. And in everything that happens, He intends that His children come to know Him, come back to Him and receive life from Him. This life is not going to be living on earth but living in heaven. Everything on earth will pass away, but everything in heaven will last forever.

Now I know why my intuition told me that many questions about life could be answered when I came to the ocean. Actually, it's not the ocean but God who gives answers to all people. God knows my thoughts and everyone's thoughts. He knows what we're thinking of and what we're asking for. When people come to the seaside with their burdens and ask for help, God grants them what they have asked for according to what they've called out for in their hearts.

That's why lovers are filled with more passion, the lonely feel cared for, and the despairing become hopeful. That's why those who suffer are hurting no more, the angry ones find peace, and the homesick are comforted. Everything comes from God. He puts the past behind us and gives us a future with a brand new beginning.

Chapter 9

A NEW BEGINNING

B ert and I cut short our vacation from seven days to three days because I was so shaken up. I wanted to leave the island that had made my heart tremble. I was anxious to go back to the city where I had come from. I wanted to leave my old lifestyle, and I had determined to become a new person.

We arrived at the Sanya Airport early. There was no one else in the waiting room. When the small airplane took off, Bert and I were the only passengers again, and I understood then that the journey had been arranged especially for me so that I would never forget what a great miracle God had performed in my life. When the small airplane took off, I looked down at the blue sea with deep feeling. During the three days that I stayed on this island, my life was like a fantasy. In this fantasy, I came to the heaven of my dreams, but I had never expected to face death.

In this death, I had experienced something unusual. I had seen God and had heard His amazing voice. Before I came to Sanya, my heart had been lonely and empty, but as I was leaving, I was rich on the inside, filled with God. I had never believed in this God before, yet He loved me so deeply and had saved my life. Because of Him, everything had changed.

I had made a promise to myself when I flew to Sanya. I had said, "I will warmly embrace every day. I will cherish every moment. I will engrave the memory in my mind and cherish it forever." During those three days, I don't know how many times I had seen God's image and heard His voice. But the fact was that I didn't embrace every moment there. Instead, every moment embraced me! I didn't want to engrave this experience in my mind or remember it forever, but God commanded me to keep this experience in my mind and cherish it forever.

When I flew away from Sanya, I made myself two promises. First, I would return to my hometown to see my parents and daughter as soon as possible. Secondly, I would go to Chengdu, the city where I was living to search for the God I saw in my vision. I wanted to know everything about Him. At that moment, I truly understood what it meant to be impatient to get home. My life should have been lost in the ocean. However, because of God, I could go home alive. This was the second time that life had been given to me by God, so I must cherish it. I hadn't been a good daughter before; I had said and done many things contrary to my parent's wishes. Now I wanted to make it up to them, honor them, and be a good daughter.

We landed in Haikou Airport, and then another airplane took us back to Chengdu. At Chengdu I parted ways with Bert, and continued on my journey alone to my hometown. When I saw my familiar hometown, the old building in which my parents lived, and my three-year-old daughter rushing down to me from the fourth floor with a big smile on her face to welcome me home, I could no longer control myself and began to cry. I held her small body close to my chest. Her beautiful smile and pure love had supported my frantic struggle in the sea. I could lose everything in this world (money, power, or prestige), I could go without having a lover to love or to be loved by, but I could not live without my daughter. I would willingly give up anything and everything for her.

When we divorced, the house, furniture, and everything else had belonged to my husband. I had nothing except my daughter. After the divorce, thinking about the life ahead of me, I had felt scared, hopeless, and disappointed. I had dared not face the future, nor had I known how. Unfortunately, my daughter and I had been together less. I had failed in my duties, but from now on everything would change. This was a new beginning. I was no longer afraid of the future, and I would be a better mother.

"Mom, you are crying. Let me wipe away all your tears," Wei Wei said. My daughter stretched out her tiny little fingers and gently wiped away my tears. She was such a cute child. Even though she had lost an intact family when she was young, she still knew how to love and care for others. Her action comforted me greatly and made me feel so gratified. I decided to be brave. No matter how poor I might be, even if I had to live by picking up litter, collecting scraps, and eating only porridge every day, I would try my best to help her have a good future. I would cry out to God. He was sure to help me and strengthen me.

"Mom isn't crying. Mom is so glad to see you," I said. I smiled at her and thought about Sanya and the struggle I had had in the sea, about how God had appeared to me and saved me just in time, and about how dangerous it was. I had been so close to leaving her with regret forever. I would not have had the chance to enjoy the warmth of being with her again. I dared not think about it any further. But I thought to myself, *From now on I will teach her how to use new eyes, to see the God who had saved me through the sun and the moon, mountains and rivers, wind and rain, frost and snow, the summer and the spring, and the autumn and the winter.*

God changed the way I thought and my attitude about life. I shared the housework with my parents such as shopping, cooking, washing dishes, sweeping the floor, and emptying the trash, and I spent all my time with my daughter. I could tell my mother was very pleased. She could tell I was changed. Many times I noticed she wanted to ask me why and how, but I kept silent. Many times I wanted to tell her, but I didn't open my mouth. In our little town, we had never heard anyone talk about God, let alone see Him. Almost everyone who knew me was aware that I had been divorced after delivering my child, and had gone through a serious emotional struggle, which made me depressed and uncommunicative. In particular, my parents were worried that I would never get over it and might become mentally disturbed. If I suddenly told them that I had gone to Sanya, had almost lost my life, and had seen God who then saved my life, they would think I was insane for sure.

They knew I had no money, they would ask, "How did you go to Sanya? Who did you go with?" How could I answer them? If I lied, it would be recorded in that scroll, and it would become another sin to account for when I died. I dared not. If I told them the truth, they would be disappointed and ashamed; they are conservative people. Looking at Mom's wrinkled face and Dad's haggard figure, I could not bear to let them worry about me any more.

"I'll wait for a while and tell them later," I said to myself. Yet in my mind, I had many unanswered questions about God. *What's His name? What does His face look like? How could a beam of light go through the palm of His hand? Is there a book that tells about Him? If there is one, which book is that? What does God talk about in that book? Where can I find it?*

With all of these questions in mind, I started my journey back to Chengdu in order to fulfill the second promise I had made on the plane when I was leaving Sanya. I desperately wanted to find out the answers but didn't know where to start.

Chapter 10

LOOKING FOR THE BIBLE

I recalled that in foreign movies I had seen people walk into church and ask for God's help when they were suffering. I had always joked about the idea and had never believed there was anything to it. Now, not only did I believe, but I also thought those people who called upon God were smart and extraordinary; they knew where to go to ask for real help. Then I thought of my American friend, Doug, and his group. I had met them three weeks before I went to Sanya.

At that time, I had just graduated from an evening English school. My teacher, Charlie, told me an American group was coming to Chengdu for a three-week visit during the summer holidays, and they were going to learn about the local culture and life. Charlie asked if I would like to be the leader of this group and along with some other graduates like me. All I needed to do was to take all of them to different teagardens and enjoy tea with them. He said it was a great opportunity to practice speaking English, and that I shouldn't miss out. I readily accepted the task, and that's how I came to know Doug.

There are many teagardens in Chengdu, and I took them to a different one each day. It seemed strange to me that each of these six Americans always had a very kind smile on their face and glowed with an indefinable happiness. No matter where they were, the minute they sat down everyone would pull out a book and take turns to read it. Sometimes one person read, and then they communicated with one another. Sometimes they sang songs together with guitar accompaniment, and I had never heard melodies that were that beautiful before.

Religion was a sensitive topic where I came from, and I had never heard anyone talk about it. What I heard was that Chinese people were not allowed to talk about religion with foreigners in public because it was against the law. Each time the Americans started to read that book, we felt we had to leave. I often cast my eyes on that book and wanted to know its contents. I wanted to know why it made them so happy. I wanted to ask, but I was ashamed of my very limited English at the time, and I was also afraid of being looked down upon for not knowing. It seemed that the group never noticed my interest in that book, and no one explained anything to me.

However, my curiosity increased, and I had more desire to know about the book. One day, after they were gone, I learned from the assistant leader that the book was called the Bible. It was about God, and all Christians read it. I thought perhaps reading the Bible was just a part of white culture. It made me wonder what "Christian" meant. I had asked the assistant leader, but he hadn't known either, so I stopped asking. Three weeks later, when the group was leaving, Doug invited me to spend the last weekend with them before their departure. He indicated that it would be a very special and meaningful gathering, but I didn't go. Instead, I went to Sanya with Bert, which takes us back to the beginning of this story.

I thought to myself, *Apparently, God must be in church and in the Bible, and I had to find Him.* One weekend in the morning, I mounted a pedicab and told the driver, "Take me to a church, please."

"What kind of church, and where is it?" Asked the driver.

"Aren't churches all the same? Are their different kinds?" I responded and I was greatly surprised.

"Of course," he said, "there are Roman Catholic churches and Christian churches. Which one are you talking about?" Asked the driver.

I was rather embarrassed. As a highly educated person, I didn't even know what a pedicab driver on the street knew. "Do you know what the difference between them is?" I responded by asking him.

"I don't know. I am just a pedicab driver, how would I know?" The driver looked at me and shook his head.

I said, "Then take me to the one you've been to."

The driver said, "I have never been to church, but I have taken someone there."

"Then take me to the Christian church," I said without thinking. In fact, I had no idea what it meant.

The driver peddled me to a church located at Shuncheng Street. It was the first time in my life that I had seen a church. Was this what a church looked like? It didn't look like something special at all. It was on my way to work every day. Why had I never noticed it? I was too timid to go inside, so I hid behind the entrance wall and peeked in. When I heard someone speaking, I quickly drew my head back.

A moment later, a woman in a black robe walked out of the entrance. She was talking with two men. After they finished talking and the two men went away, the woman saw me leaning against the wall.

"May I help you?" she asked kindly. The smile on her face put me at ease.

"Nothing special. I just want to buy a Bible." My voice was low, and my heart was beating fast. I was afraid that she would ask the reason why I wanted to buy this book.

"Sorry, but we are sold out of Bibles," she said.

"Oh, may I ask at which bookstore I can buy it?" I didn't want to give up.

"It's not sold in any bookstore. You can only buy it at a church. Normally we sell it during Christmas time," said the woman.

"What do you mean? What is Christmas? When is that?" I was rather embarrassed to ask these questions; they made me look uninformed and ignorant.

The woman responded, "Christmas is the time to celebrate the birth of Jesus. It's on December 24th and 25th."

I thought she must have misunderstood what I was looking for. I was looking for the Bible, not Jesus. I repeated my request one more time. The woman smiled and said, "Yes, if you come in the middle of December, it should be available." She was patient, and I felt a little comforted. Oh, what a long time to wait! It was the middle of August and Christmas was more than four months away! I left the church with great disappointment.

I started the very long period of waiting after I went home. It was only four months, yet it seemed that I spent my entire life waiting. In those days, I lived in an unfinished apartment owned by Auntie Meng's daughter. Auntie Meng was a classmate of my father's from his childhood who had moved to Chengdu many years ago. Her daughter was going to have a baby and needed more care from the family, so she moved back in with them. Auntie Meng's whole family was made up of wonderful people with very kind hearts, and they all sympathized with the difficult position I was in after my divorce. Her daughter and son-in-law allowed me to stay in their new apartment on the seventh floor for free.

I had one single bed, one chair provided by my friends, and some very basic cooking utensils. There was no phone, no TV, and no computer, but this was my home, a home for only one person. It was an unfinished apartment in a new building. No one had done any of the woodwork or furnishing in it, and no one had moved in, so the whole building was empty. I was almost the only one going up and down the stairs. I went out to look for a job on my bicycle during the daytime and stayed at home in the evening, but I didn't feel lonely and wasn't frightened.

I knew I wasn't alone, but the Holy Spirit was with me all the time. If He could save me in the sea, He could also protect me in this big building. I talked with Him happily every day and asked Him for all kinds of things. I even asked Him which route to take when I went out or came home. I didn't know which way was going to have busy traffic, but He knew. I could not see which road was free, but He could. The Holy Spirit became my best friend and closest companion during that time. People often saw me pushing a broken bicycle and talking to myself, and they all looked at me strangely. Only I knew that I wasn't a madwoman. I was communicating with the very real Holy Spirit. They could not see Him, but I could.

Finally, December came and I bought my first Bible. For me, this book was holy and precious because it talked about God. After purchasing the book, I went directly home and devoured it. As soon as I opened the Bible, I learned God's name is Yahweh. I immediately believed the stories about all the creations He had done and all the miracles He had performed in the Old Testament. However, the other parts of the Bible I couldn't understand very well even though the words were simple. I read the whole Old Testament in search of a passage that would describe God's face and hands as I saw Him in my vision, but I found nothing to describe God's face and hands and

I was so disappointed. I thought I must have missed the passage so I reread the Old Testament again. I still didn't find a description of God's face and His hands.

I wondered, *Hasn't anyone seen God? When Moses was with Him face-to-face, why didn't he describe what God looked like? But I had seen Him. Indeed, I had seen Him. He is Spirit formed in the image of a man, and He appeared to me larger than life. He saved me, and I can never forget that. However, where are the words describing His folded wings, the brilliant, bright light behind Him, His bleeding heart, and His hands? Why could a beam of light go through His hand?* I was very confused and even started to question if this book was the one I was looking for.

When I turned the page over to the New Testament, I had more difficulty in understanding it. It talked about the family tree of Jesus Christ, but who was Jesus? What does Christ mean? Why does the book talk about the family tree of Jesus? The Bible is supposed to be a holy book! It should be about God, but why did it have Jesus in it? Placing Jesus in the book meant making Him equal to God, but the God that I saw came from heaven, how could a human be equal to God? Moreover, is a person's family tree really important? I was even more confused. I didn't understand the family tree of Jesus, and I lost interest in the New Testament and stopped reading it. I put away the Bible for over a year, but my heart never stopped searching for the true God and calling upon His name.

I didn't dare tell anyone about my experience. I never went to church or asked other people whether they had ever seen God. I didn't know whom to ask. I was hungry for the answers, but I didn't know where they could be found. In those days, I only had God with me, so I appealed to Him: "Almighty God, you appeared to me before and now you gave me this book, but I do not understand it. It's up to you to teach me who Jesus is and why He is in your book. If you are not going to appear to me or speak to me again, please send someone to teach me. I am eager to know everything about you."

God knew what was in my heart and He heard my prayer. A few months later, He led Doug back to Chengdu, and this time he wasn't only staying for three weeks but for many years. Doug was always very enthusiastic and loved to help others. When he observed young people like me who had a strong desire to learn English, he invited us to a free English study group at his dorm room. We would get together each Friday evening. We started by reading one-page essays written in English, and then we read someone's entire life story. His name was Jesus.

Before we started, Doug summarized the story for us: "Jesus was born to the Virgin Mary, and was conceived by the Holy Spirit. He is the only begotten Son of God. He is the Word become flesh who came into the world. He was born to take away our sins. He loved all the people in the world, but He was crucified. He shed His blood for our sins and died on the cross. Three days later, He was raised from the dead and appeared to His disciples. Now He is at the right hand of the Father and has authority to judge the whole world."

I really wasn't interested at all in this story about Jesus and I thought it was a fabricated story. I just saw the Friday evening as a language learning opportunity. I thought to myself, *These people really know how to make up stories. Just let them talk about whatever they want. I'm here to study English. Wait till the study is finished, and I will tell them my story and talk about the real God.* In my heart, the man who had appeared in the ocean and had saved my life was the real God.

Later on Doug told us repeatedly, "Jesus is God, the only true God who loves the world. He cures the sick and casts out devils. He has performed many wonders and miracles." Doug always became very fervent each time when he talked about this, as if the story was true. It bothered me a lot, and several times I decided to stop going to his dorm for the meetings. However, each time, there was a mysterious power always drawing me back to Doug's place. I could not resist that power for it gave me a hungry heart. My hungry heart looked forward to each Friday evening.

One day we started to read about the disciple Thomas in the Gospel of John. Thomas didn't believe that Jesus was God. He said, "Unless I see the nail marks in his hands and put my finger where the nails were, and put my hand into his side, I will not believe it." (John 20:25) Jesus said to Thomas, "Put your finger here; see my hands. Reach out your hand and put it into my side. Stop doubting

86

and believe." (John 20:26) Thomas replied, "My Lord and my God!" Then Jesus told him, "Because you have seen me, you have believed; blessed are those who have not seen and yet have believed." (John 20:27–29) I realized I was like Thomas; I had a doubting heart.

Doug pointed his left index finger to the palm of this right hand and his right index finger to the palm of his left hand. He said, "Because of love, the King of Kings and the Lord of Lords was crucified. However, three days later, not only was He raised from the dead, but He also appeared to His disciples in different places. As for the mark of the nails in His hands, the disciples saw it, and Thomas touched it. Everything was true."

Doug's gesture reminded me of the light passing through the palm of God's hands. I had seen that twice when He was in front of me in my vision in the sea. Since that day, I frequently looked at my hands and asked myself, "How could light pass through the palm of His hands unless there was a hole in the middle? But how could that be?" I looked at all the people around me and found that no one had a hole in their hands. "Could that be the difference between a man's hands and God's?" I had this question in mind and never stopped searching for the answers. Now, the answer was right in front of me. It was in the New Testament of the Bible, which I had stopped reading a year before.

"I have seen that hand," I said to myself. Suddenly, I trembled all over. I felt something extremely powerful pass through my whole body like waves of an electric current. I could not even sit properly.

I quickly put my hands on the arms of the wooden chair so that I wouldn't fall from it. I had experienced this same feeling many times before. Whenever I recalled the Lord appearing to me in the sea, I felt this way. It wasn't the first time it happened, but it had never been so strong.

I tried to not let anyone else in the group notice what was happening to me. When the study finished that night, I walked out from Doug's dorm room to my home. As I was walking I asked myself many times, was Jesus really the God who saved me in Sanya?

Chapter 11

FINDING JESUS CHRIST

Soon after that night at Doug's dorm room, I started to re-read the stories about Jesus in the New Testament. However, I could not let Him come into my heart because of my stubbornness. In my heart, I only had the God who had appeared to me and had saved my life in the ocean. He had come down on a cloud. His image, the brilliant bright light behind Him, His blood, His voice, and everything about Him often appeared before me. I was sure He was from above. Only He could do wonders and miracles, only He knew the hearts of all people, only He was the true God, and others were not. Although I had these strong convictions, I could not put the Bible down. The Bible held me like a magnet. I liked to read it when I had nothing to do.

One cloudy morning in November 1997, before I went out, I finished reading how Jesus made the blind see, the deaf hear, the lame walk, and hunchbacks straight. He cured lepers and called the dead Lazarus out from a tomb. I shook my head and said aloud, "Jesus, if you really are God, you can perform many wonders and miracles. Please perform one for me on this very normal day, and then I will believe you are the One." I thought to myself, *I didn't request this until the moment I was going out. Jesus will not have enough time to perform a miracle even if He wanted to.*

I left home on time riding my bicycle. I had just become a salesperson and was going to a hospital to promote medicines and inquire about the hospital's medical needs. Around 11:30 a.m., after finishing my business, a thought flashed through my mind when I was approaching the gate to leave the hospital. *Where was the miracle? I didn't see one.* Then I saw a group of more than ten people. Four of them were carrying a stretcher, and the others followed. On the stretcher lay a young man.

Before I could see them clearly, they had disappeared into the building that I had just left. I continued to push my bicycle on my way out. It was almost lunchtime, and I was thinking about where to go and what to eat. When I approached the gate, I suddenly stopped, looked back, and then followed them. I was never someone who liked to join in on something without being invited. I didn't know why I stopped and followed them.

"What happened?" I asked one of the men.

"The Buddha was watching out for this fellow," the man said. "This young guy was really fortunate. In all of the years I have been alive I have never seen anything like this before. He fell from the sixth floor, and there's nothing wrong with him."

Then I asked for more information and got the whole story. This fellow was a cleaner. When he was cleaning the windows on the sixth floor, he slipped and fell to the ground. Everyone in the building heard a huge noise. They all thought that a bag of sand had hit the ground. They never guessed it was a person.

The directors of the company were terrified and hurried down to investigate the situation outside. Defying everyone's expectation, the young man stood up and said he was fine, which made the directors even more afraid. They called the workers and commanded them to put the young man on a stretcher and take him to the nearest hospital for a checkup. It would be terrible if he lost his life. The doctors examined the young man carefully and found no bleeding inside or outside his body. Not a single bone was broken. The doctors didn't believe the black-and-white X-rays which showed nothing was abnormal, so they ordered more X-rays, in color this time. They still found nothing wrong with the young man. All the people present said the young fellow was extremely lucky, probably because his ancestors' burial location had been chosen well, and that when he returned home he should burn more incense to Buddha and give thanks to the Goddess of Mercy.

Not believing them, I walked into the doctor's room and asked, "Is it true that this person really has nothing wrong with him?"

The doctor, who knew me, said, "We didn't find anything unusual except that one blood index was much higher. This is the first time I've seen such a thing after many years of working here. It's truly amazing."

"Is that normal when the blood index is higher?" I asked the doctor.

"When human beings meet an emergency situation like this, the body tries to protect itself, so it is considered normal when the blood index goes much higher," said the doctor.

Then I went up to the young fellow. He was lying on the bed close to the right side of the door of the doctor's room. "How old are you?" I asked him.

"Twenty-six," he said, but he looked younger.

"How do you feel now?" I asked him again.

"I am fine, just a little bit dizzy," he answered.

His face was rather pale. *How could he not feel dizzy after falling from such a high building? I would pass out just from horror,* I thought to myself.

"Have a good rest and you will be all right," I said to the young fellow.

"Thank you." He was very appreciative of my kind words.

"You are welcome." I smiled at him and left the room.

I pushed my bicycle along as I left the hospital, but then stopped at the gate. I thought to myself, *The fact that this young man's life was saved had nothing to do with the Buddha or the location of his ancestor's grave, or the Goddess of Mercy. If it wasn't a mighty hand*

*catching his falling body in time and if it wasn't the true God pro-
tecting him, how could he be safe? It was the true God who saved his
life. However, this group of people could not see it, and they gave all
the glory to Buddha, which has no life or spirit, and to the Goddess
of Mercy, which could not even move an inch. How blind and how
ungrateful they are! Well at least I am no longer like that.*

Suddenly I remembered the promise I had made to Jesus before
I had left home: "If you show me a miracle today, I will believe you
are the real God." Jesus was alive! I exclaimed in my heart. He had
really heard my promise and had shown me a miracle! Looking at
the sky, I said, "Jesus, is it really you? Are you speaking to me, and
do you want me to believe it was you who appeared in the sea?" I
started to have some feelings about Jesus. I went home happily and
read the Bible for a long time.

What had happened on that day made my relationship with Jesus
closer. I started to spend more time reading the Bible. However, I
still had unanswered questions. *Jesus was born to Mary as a human.
How could He be God? It's so hard to understand people. How could
a mere human being read people's minds? But, if Jesus isn't God,
how could He have heard my words before I left? Since nothing is
a coincidence, it must have God's purpose in it. But what indeed is
God trying to tell me?*

In December of 1998, I was in a hospital for the treatment of
hemorrhoids, which I'd had since the birth of my daughter. I was

half-believing, but then Jesus took away all of my remaining resistance and doubts and I came to Him.

My hemorrhoids often bled and became worse and worse. This condition directly influenced my daily life and dragged me down. I decided to have them removed. The operation was arranged for the day before Christmas. I didn't tell my parents in my hometown because they were looking after my daughter and things were hard enough. I didn't want them to worry about me. I also didn't tell my friends. I thought I had God with me, and I would be okay soon enough without friends taking care of me. That cold winter day, I had the operation in the hospital affiliated with the Chengdu University of Traditional Chinese Medicine.

To my surprise, the second day after the operation, Doug brought a group of people to the ward to visit me. I only knew some of them. They sat around my sickbed and shared the love of Jesus with me. They sang to me, talked, and laughed with me. They brought smiles and happiness when they came and left blessings and peace when they left. I was so touched that I could not hold back my tears.

I had thought I was going to spend seven days alone in the hospital. I didn't expect such care. We had no blood relationship, but all of them gave up their precious time, took a crowded bus to visit me in the hospital, and made me feel less lonely. They had even brought me some spiritual books, a tape recorder with batteries in it, taped gospel music, and earphones, so I could read books during the day when I got bored, and lie down and listen to music when I got tired.

I will never forget a song called "Flowers of the Field." I don't remember how many times I listened to it. The lyrics were very simple:

Flowers of the field are dressed in bright array
Birds in the heavens never worry for a day
Our gracious Father watches over all
He cares so much for us that He will never let us fall
All of our needs our Father already knows
In stress or trials, great mercy He bestows
Our gracious Father watches day by day
He is Almighty God
Believe in Him, He'll show you the way

The melody was beautiful, and the voice was so pleasant. It was as if a voice from heaven leisurely walked into my mind, and it was as if Jesus was really whispering in my ears. What was He trying to tell me? I opened the New Testament at my bedside, and these words caught my attention: "Therefore I tell you, do not worry about your life. What you will eat or drink; or about your body, what you will wear. Is not life more important than food, and the body more important than clothes? Look at the birds of the air; they do not sow or reap or store away in barns, and yet your heavenly Father feeds them. Are you not much more valuable than they?" (Matt. 6: 25–26) I was touched by this passage and felt that God was speaking to my heart that He loves the world and loves everything that He created.

He has always given without being stingy, not only to the birds in the sky but also to all the animals of the forest and livestock on numerous mountains. They all depend on Him for food.

Besides that, God loves me more than He loves any of these. The passage reminded me of the God that I had seen in the sea in Sanya. True love had shown in His eyes. His love had never departed from me. Because of love, He tolerated my sins and bore the pain of bleeding. Because of love, He prepared Himself for me, so that I could gain a new life because of Him. *There is only one true God in this world. He is the One that I saw. I have trusted in Him and have faith in Him. Jesus, are you Him?* This was the only question that I asked frequently after I heard this song and read this passage.

On the fourth day after the operation, I read another story from a spiritual book. There was a poor family that often did not have enough food to eat. One day, George, the man of the house, prayed to the Lord: "Please give us a few fish so that my children won't say 'We ran out of food again.'" Just after he had finished praying, someone knocked at the door. George opened the door and saw a stranger standing outside. He gave the family a big fish and left in a hurry without leaving his name. George then bowed face down to the ground and gave thanks to the Lord.

When I was reading this, I thought that my situation was similar. I had hired a middle-aged woman to take care of me in the hospital during the first three days after the operation. In China it's common to hire a person who can provide day care while a patient is in the hospital. This lady I hired had provided food, made herbal tea, and helped me in and out of the bed and to the bathroom. This kind of help is typically not part of the nurse's daily duty. Unfortunately, day care was very expensive, and I couldn't afford it. I had thought that by the fourth day, I should be able to take care of myself and go down to the first floor for food. On the fourth day, I let her go home.

Contrary to my expectations, I was much weaker than I thought. Although I could get out of bed and walk around a bit, the wounds were still very painful. It was impossible for me to go down seven flights of stairs to get food, and I didn't know anybody in this big hospital building. I was starving and felt dizzy, and the only choice I had was to lie down and sleep.

My stomach was empty, and I could not sleep, so I remembered the story I had just read, as well as the story in the Bible about Jesus feeding five thousand people. I thought, *Jesus, if you really are God, you know my situation. You know how hungry I am and how badly I need food. Please provide me some food. It doesn't need to be a lot, just a little bit for my stomach would be enough. Didn't you feed five thousand before? But now, only one person needs to be fed. Isn't that much easier than feeding five thousand? If you really give me some food, then I will believe you are the true God.* Although I was testing Jesus, I really hoped that He would realize my need, because at that moment no one else knew I was starving except the true God.

I had been lying there for a long time when I felt someone shaking my body. "Little Li, Little Li, get out of bed." When I opened my eyes, I saw the old woman who was in the bed next to mine. We had the same condition, and she had come to the hospital for the same reason, but she was still waiting for the operation. She stood next to my bed with a big splendid smile on her face. In her left hand, she was holding a yellow plastic food box.

The old woman spoke really loud, "I had already ordered my lunch in the hospital today, but my daughter-in-law sent me another one. This one I ordered is yours now. Eat it up before it gets cold. Look, it has stir-fried liver, and won't taste good when it gets cold."

"Didn't she know you had made the order?" I asked her, sitting up and putting on my clothes.

"Yes, she knew. She said that all of a sudden she had a strong desire to cook for me. My daughter-in-law really cares for me. I am so blessed," said the old woman happily.

"When did this happen?" I asked the woman after I had finished dressing.

"About forty five minutes ago. Go ahead and eat your food." The old woman persisted in giving me her food box with great enthusiasm.

Jesus is the true God indeed! I exclaimed in my heart. I ate and thought, *Jesus prepared this meal for me before I had even started to ask. He knows my mind and my thoughts. He heard the cry from the depths of my heart and responded quickly. He knows exactly where I am and what I need. Not only that, He saved the young fellow's life so that he had no broken bones. Jesus did all the things that only the true God could do. Who else would He be except God Himself? Jesus is the true God who appeared to me before. In fact, this is the truth that the Lord has been trying to tell me during these days.* Finally, I accepted Jesus as my Lord.

Doug said, "Jesus is love, and love needs to be shared." This group of people carried out that love and brought it into my hospital ward. On those cold winter days, this love was like sunshine and a warm breeze. It warmed my icy heart and blew off the fog before my eyes. This love was like a charcoal fire in the snow and a small gentle rain; it melted the high wall in my heart and moistened the parched soul. This love was like lamps in the night that shine for those returning from a long voyage. It made me see the way to reach the destination.

After my divorce, my wandering heart finally found its harbor in the love of Jesus. In this harbor, I relearned the meaning of the words wait, hope, expect, and dream. I waited for Doug's group to show up more often and hoped for hearing the sounds of their footsteps. I went into the corridors of the hospital and dreamed that time itself had stopped. I expected the happiness to stay forever. Doug and some of the group came to visit me every other day, bringing joy and peace and leaving beautiful memories. I wished the ward were my home and that I would never have to leave.

I had sought the Bible and the true God, but had never expected to find the Lord Jesus. Through my sickness, Jesus opened my understanding. Ever since then, His name has come into my heart, and stayed within my soul. I started to re-examine my life. Jesus Christ gave me my first life, yet I was forlorn, depressed, and miserable because I didn't know Him. Now He gave me a second chance to live. My next question was how should I hold on to it and make it meaningful.

Chapter 12

I KNEW WHO WAS IN
CHARGE OF THE FUTURE

*M*y concept of life changed completely after I met Jesus. Death for me was not a threat, and life to me meant hope. The Bible says that Jesus is the only true and living God. Whoever believes in Him will live forever. I often thought to myself, *When I finish my journey in this world and my body returns to dust, I want my soul to go to heaven and forever be with Him. Wherever Jesus is, that's where I want to be. However, I am a woman who hasn't been baptized yet. Can I still be accepted into heaven? Although I have accepted Jesus into my heart, I don't know the Bible very well. Can I still be baptized and become a disciple?* I wasn't sure, so I kept asking the Holy Spirit.

One day in January 1999, I was riding my bicycle home. Suddenly, the Holy Spirit spoke to me: "Be a Christian, be a Christian." I repeated what I had heard and asked the Holy Spirit, "Who is a Christian around me?" At that moment, I was passing by my friend Doug's school building, then I thought about him. *Is he a Christian?* I wasn't sure. He had never said that he was, but I still made up my mind to go to see him. I thought to myself, *If he is excited at what I am going to tell him, that means he is. And if he is at home, that means this idea to become a Christian really is from God. If he's not at home, then it's not.* I had decided to not call him before going to his place like I used to do. Instead I went to his place directly without an appointment. I wanted to give him a surprise.

I arrived and knocked at his door. The door opened at once, and Doug stood there. I said to him before he started talking, "I want to be a Christian!" He had been surprised to see me standing outside his door. After hearing what I said, his eyes grew large with wonder, and his mouth dropped opened. He was astonished with joy. After he composed himself, he gave me a big hug. "Now, we are brother and sister in Christ. Welcome! Welcome!" He let me go and then hugged me again. It was such a peaceful, warm moment, and I felt I had come home.

After a long while, Doug noticed we were still standing outside. "I'm so sorry. I'm overjoyed, and I forgot to invite you to come in. Please, come in now." He let me walk into his small dorm room and sat me down next to the window. He turned around and made two cups of Chinese tea. Then he sat opposite me. I saw the door wasn't completely shut but rather half-opened. He always did that to let me know that when I was with him alone, it was totally safe. He really was a man with high morals, and I had never met anyone like him.

"Thank the Lord," Doug said. "Mei, it's so wonderful that you have come. I have been so busy with my studies recently. I just finished my tests yesterday. I felt so tired and had planned to have a good rest today without seeing anyone. I had decided to have a good sleep and even unhooked the telephone line. I didn't expect to hear a knock at the door. I got up at once without thinking and opened the door, and it was you. You told me you wanted to be a Christian, and I was so happy and forgot to welcome you in. Praise the Lord! Indeed, the Lord arranged this!" He had a sip of tea. His face was one big sincere smile, and I believed everything he said.

He put down the teacup and said, "Now, can you share with me what has happened?" Doug could not hide his excitement.

"I was riding my bicycle," I said. "Suddenly, the Holy Spirit touched me, and I wanted to be a Christian, so I came to you."

"And why do you believe in God?" Doug asked.

I knew that he wasn't trying to invade my privacy. He only wanted to know more about why I had changed my faith. "He saved my life. I was drowning, and I closed my eyes, waiting to die. Then I saw Him with my very own eyes, and He saved me, so I believe in Him." My explanation was very short, and I didn't even mention the sea in Sanya. I was ashamed to tell anyone the reason that I had gone to the beach, and I wanted my friend's image of me to remain pure.

"When did this happen?" he asked again.

"It was that summer I took you to the teagardens. Do you still remember the last weekend? You invited me for a very special gathering, but I didn't go. I went to another place, and it happened there." I tried not to explain too much.

"Oh, I see." Noticing that I wasn't ready to share my story, Doug changed the subject. "Thank the Lord. Thank the Lord. Since we met you and other students last year, we started to pray for all of you, asking the Lord to prepare your hearts. We noticed your interest in the Bible so we especially prayed for you hoping you would get to know Him. We hoped that you would find eternal life. I didn't think our prayers would be answered so quickly." The Holy Spirit had really touched Doug, and his eyes were glistening with tears.

"Now, why don't I lead you in prayer," said Doug to me.

"What is prayer?" I asked. That was a new word for me. I had never heard of it. "I don't know how," I said to him slowly.

"Prayer is talking to God and telling Him the words of your heart. It's communicating with Him," said Doug with a smile.

If that's prayer, then I know how. I speak with Him every day, I thought to myself. "But we don't need to say anything. He already knows," I said to Doug seriously.

"Yes, He already knows. However, if we pray for everything, this really pleases Him. It doesn't matter if you don't know how to pray. Just follow me, sentence by sentence." This idea comforted me. He bowed his head and with folded hands started to pray for me: "Heavenly Father, we worship you, praise you, and thank you.

Because of your wonderful work, you brought Mei to yourself today. Please forgive all her sins, seen and unseen, all the things she has done wrong or she hasn't done yet but will do wrong. Please forgive them all. Please accept her into your kingdom, your eternal dwelling place in heaven, for she wishes to follow you for the rest of her life, and to walk the way you want her to walk. Please guide her, bless her future, and let everything she is going to do be done in your way. This prayer is in the name of our Lord Jesus Christ. Amen."

It was not until then, that I, an atheist, came to know why I had been saved by God. Indeed, these believers from the United States had been praying behind my back that I'd be saved and had asked Christ to forgive all my sins. They had asked Jesus to have mercy on me, to love me, and to open my heart, eyes, and ears, so that I could know Him, see Him, hear His voice, experience His incredible love, and enter His kingdom.

This was the love of Christ. Time couldn't stop it, and distance couldn't hinder it. There weren't any boundaries He couldn't cross. This was the love of Christ. It saw no difference in race, gender, or language. Anybody at any time, in any location could come to Him and pray, and Christ had always been focused on His children and listened to their prayers, never stopping for a moment.

In June 1999, the Holy Spirit touched me, and I wanted to be baptized. I found Doug again. He was very happy but said to me, "I am not a registered pastor in China. I shouldn't be the one to baptize you, but I know people who can. There is a couple who love the Lord deeply, and they live close by. In fact, you have seen them before. This will only be known between you and me, and there is no need to tell others now." I understood him and promised.

A few days later, Doug took me to the couple's home. Indeed, I had seen them before. They had come to visit me with Doug when I was in the hospital. This wonderful couple welcomed me with great enthusiasm and big smiles on their faces. Pastor Li could have risked going to jail by baptizing me in their very simple, rented home. In this way I came to the Lord Jesus Christ. From then on, my name was written in the Book of Life, and I would have eternal life because of my faith in Him.

In that small room, the Lord and His Holy Spirit was with the four of us. Pastor Li and his wife gently hummed a song for me, which was often sung at baptisms, "One day I dedicated myself to Jesus and I follow His guidance with a pure heart. How wonderful! I will never forget this happy day, happy day. I will never forget this day." My heart was filled with peace and happiness, hope and enthusiasm.

Yes, I would never forget this day. It was so special and meaningful. It drew me closer to the Lord. And it reminded me of another unforgettable day, the day Jesus had appeared to me in the Sanya sea. The day I had struggled with life, faced death, and given up in my desperation; The day that Jesus Christ had shown His almighty power, and made the blind see and the deaf hear; the day He had saved my life and given me hope; and also the day when an old life had died, yet a new life had been born.

I have trusted and followed the Lord since the day I saw Him. On the day of my baptism I reconfirmed my decision, and that decision hasn't changed and it never will. Who was I? I was nobody—nobody yesterday, nobody today, and nobody tomorrow. It was Christ who chose me, picked me up out of the dust heap and from the garbage, and cleansed me. With His mighty potter's hands, He refashioned me from being dirt and rubble. He gave me the direction of life and made my life meaningful. I found my value in Him and I put my trust in Him, because I knew who was in charge of the future.

Haikou Airport

Arriving at Sanya Airport

The view of Da Dong Hai Beach from the hotel room

The first time of my life stepping into the ocean

Playing in the surf on beautiful
Dadonghai Beach

Back in the hotel room after my near
death experience and vision

On my way to find the young fellow who took me out of ocean

The local lifeguard who pulled me out of the ocean

Dinner with the lifeguard and his best friend

Leaving Sanya on the third day of the trip

Waiting to board the plane at Sanya airport

*No other passengers
on the airplane*

Family Photo took in May 2000 on my grandmother's birthday: Me, the author-Last row, far right; My father-Front row, far right with my cousin's son; My mother-Middle row, third from right; My cousin Lulu-Last row, second from left; Lulu's husband-Last row, far left; My uncle-Front row, second from right with Lulu's daughter, Yang; My aunt-Front row, second from left with my daughter, Weiwei infront; My grandmother-First row in the middle with a baby in front

*Graham and WeiWei at our
home in Los Angeles*

*Mei, Graham and WeiWei,
a new family in Los Angeles*

Mei and WeiWei

Chapter 13

WHEN I WAS BORN,
HE BLESSED ME

After I was baptized, I began to think about my past in a different way. The past stays the same, but my perspective on it has changed. In every part of my journey and at each step in my life, I saw the Lord's love for me. His grace was indeed with me all along.

In June 1969, I was born into a small family of three, my parents and my older sister. The Four of us lived in a little town by the Yangtze River in Chongqing, China. When I was born, my mother lacked milk to feed me, and I wouldn't drink cow's milk. When my mother fed me cow's milk, it would always come right back out of my mouth and nose. My mother was anxious and cried, "What is to be done? She is hungry but has no milk she can drink, and she cries herself hoarse. At this rate, she will starve to death. What can I do?"

At that time the family was poor, and my parents both were ordinary workers with very low salaries. Where could they get breast milk even if they had money?

My mother didn't know what to do. She didn't know Jesus, the Living God, who made manna fall from the sky and the hungry were fed. He ordered water to come out of the rock and the thirsty were satisfied. If Jesus could do that, He could also prepare my daily milk. As the Lord, He would not let me go hungry, since He had given me this life. When I was facing possible death as an infant He provided a miracle for me.

One day a woman called Auntie Mei walked into my town. Her newborn son had died seven days after his birth. Her breasts were swelled and filled with milk. Auntie Mei came to my town with a mission. Her mission was to search for a baby to nurse. She saw many, but she wasn't satisfied. She was just about to leave the town when she saw me in my mother's arms. She smiled and said to my mother, "Look at this baby and the spirit in her eyes. She's very smart and full of vitality. I'll take care of her." Thereafter, this young woman became my nanny.

The nanny told my parents that she didn't live far away. According to her, after crossing the Yangtze River and walking a little while, they would come to her home. My parents followed her because they wanted to see the place where I would live and to make sure that I would be safe. After they got off the boat, the nanny took them on a very long walk. They tramped over hill and dale, yet they still didn't see her home.

"Didn't you say your home was just a short walk from the river? Why haven't we arrived?" My mother was doubtful and thought this woman might be a fraud.

"Just ahead. Do you see the hill there? Go over the hill and it will be there." The way the nanny talked, she didn't seem like a fraud.

After going over that hill and then many other hills, my parents still didn't see her home. "Where is your home? How far away is it from here? Do you live there or not?" My mother started to suspect her, and she was going to take me back home. She was afraid she was being tricked by someone involved in human trafficking, and would be led to a remote place where I would be taken away.

However, the nanny assured my mother with vows and oaths. "Really, it's just ahead of us. Do not treat me like someone who would cheat you." Soon she pointed to a tree. "Do you see that tree? My house is just behind that tree."

Finally, they arrived at the nanny's home. In fact, her home was many kilometers away from my parents. There was a road but no bus. The only transportation was by foot. The nanny had tramped all that way, walked to the Yangtze River, crossed the river by boat, and walked into our town. Now she had taken me in her arms, and followed the same route back. The reason she didn't tell my parents the whole truth from the very beginning was because she loved me so much from the very first moment she saw me. Her home was in a remote village, and she was afraid that my parents would not be willing to give me away.

The nanny took me home because of her devotion. It was a simple home with peace and warmth in it. The husband was a nice, honest man, who worked for the community as an accountant. They had several children, the youngest of which had just passed away. Among all of these children, the nanny loved me the most. She would take me on her back or in her arms, and we were never apart, even when she was working on the top of a hill. I eased the pain in her heart from the loss of her son, and my presence comforted her greatly. In her eyes, I was her newborn baby, the youngest one in her home, and the one needing the most care and love.

The nanny spoiled me in every way. When I was hungry and cried, she would undo the top buttons of her blouse and nurse me. When I was tired, she would hold me in her arms until I fell asleep. She fanned me under the moonlight, carried me in the gentle breeze, and made shoes for me next to a smoky lamp. When I misbehaved, she never blamed me but only loved me, and let me continue to do things my way. Because of her unprincipled accommodation and spoiling, I became stubborn and obstinate. I had a contentious character, which caused me to rebel and resulted in reversals in my life in later years.

During this period, my parents could only visit me occasionally because of the long distance and lack of public transportation. From the beginning of my life, I was not with my parents. I didn't have the chance to enjoy my mother's sweet milk. I didn't see the smiles of my parents day after day. I didn't get their pacifier in the nights. However, the Lord Jesus had prepared the nanny's home for me. Although it was many kilometers away, I was with parents in a home. I did enjoy a mother's sweet milk. I did see the smiles of my nanny and her husband every day, and I did get their pacifier in the nights. In my own home I only had one big sister, but in my nanny's home I had six sisters and brothers.

Seven months flew by, and I grew from a nursing infant to a babbling baby. Meanwhile, the nanny gave me her sincerest and deepest love until one day the hand of Jesus took me away from her because He had prepared the nanny's loving home for another abandoned infant.

What happened was on one cold winter morning on her way to work, my real mother saw a few people in a circle, buzzing about something by the gate of an elementary school. She walked closer and saw a baby wrapped in a tattered, cotton-padded jacket lying on the ground. It seemed that the baby was still alive, but its breathing was very weak. My mother liked its beautiful, delicate eyes, so she took the baby home and handed it to my step-grandfather.

My step-grandfather opened the jacket and realized the baby was a female. Then he took a closer look at the baby and was shocked at what he saw. There was a lot of soil on her face, in her hair and nostrils, in her mouth and ears, in her nails and toes, and all over her body. My step-grandfather conjectured that a teenage girl had given birth and broken the law. She would be discriminated against and laughed at, or even go to jail. She would dare not keep the baby. Someone must have been hired to dig a pit in the ground and bury the baby while she was still alive. Thus, no one would know what had happened and the disgrace could be hidden.

Perhaps, the gravedigger felt pity for the newborn. He may have gone back to dig the baby out, wrapped her in this tattered, cotton-padded jacket, and left her at the gate of the elementary school before dawn hoping someone with a good heart would take her home. Otherwise, what else could explain so much soil on her little body?

My step-grandfather looked all over the jacket, and he found nothing except a piece of paper indicating the baby's birth date. His heart was filled with sympathy for her. At the time, my uncle and aunt had no children after many years of marriage. According to the superstitions in our town, they would have their own child very soon if they adopted one first. My step-grandfather thought to himself for a while, and then persuaded my uncle and aunt to adopt the baby and name her "Lulu," which meant, "picked up on the road."

Lulu was very thin and weak, and the family had no breast milk to feed her. My step-grandfather thought of my nanny, and he decided to exchange me for Lulu in order to keep her alive. My parents respected his decision and immediately went on their journey. They crossed the river in a boat, trekked the long distance, and reached my nanny's house to bring me home. Telephones did not exist in those days, so they could not notify my nanny beforehand. My nanny was unwilling to let me go. She had not been prepared for my departure and could not stop weeping.

In the end, my nanny packed all of my things for my journey and accompanied me out. She was afraid I would cry and scream if I didn't have milk on the way home. But in fact, it was my nanny who cried while she walked with me. This time my parents walked ahead and my nanny fell behind. She carried me all the way to the bank of the Yangtze River, where the ferry was just docking. My nanny reluctantly handed me to my mother and stood watching in tears until the boat pulled away.

That's how Jesus brought me home safely. From that time on, I never saw my nanny again. Nevertheless, this experience left an indelible mark on me for the rest of my life. At one point my father after he had had too much to drink told me why my name was really "Mei." He said, "Mei" stands for the plum flower, which only blooms in the coldest time of the winter. I was born in the Summer. The reason they gave me this first name was to remember the nanny "Auntie Mei" and how much she had done for me. Without her I would not have survived.

I deeply appreciated my nanny, yet I was even more grateful to God who prepared her for me. It was nothing else but God's mighty hand that took me away from my mother's arms and put me into my nanny's arms, from one side of the Yangtze River to the other. It was His miraculous leading that took me from a small room to an open slope, from a crowded and noisy city to a quiet and peaceful countryside. To stop my parents from worrying and to prevent me from starving, the Lord completely changed my living environment. However, His love accompanied me and that has never changed.

When my nanny was working, she placed me on the edge of the field. The Lord Jesus touched my body with the sunshine, and He kissed my face with the gentle breeze. He created music for me with the murmur of the rivers and the gurgling of the springs in the hills. He cradled me with the songs of frogs croaking in the farm and with the singing of cicadas in the trees. He brought along the fragrance of the mountain flowers and the earth for me to smell. He let me see the green hills when I opened my eyes. He let me touch the grass when I stretched out my hands. All of this brought me great delight. He granted me care, mercy, love, affection, and entertainment–everything a baby needed. He granted me abundance. Because of His blessings, I lacked nothing.

Chapter 14

WHILE I WAS GROWING UP, HE DISCIPLINED ME

*A*fter I was brought home from my nanny's house, I started a new stage of my life. While I was growing up in my hometown, God continually lavished His love and mercy on me. He put different people around me and helped me to grow as a young child.

I was thin and my skin was dark brown when I was brought home, and step-grandfather gave me a nickname "Black Shovel." Because of this name, I was often belittled by my family members and neighbors. The neighbors knew our family had adopted an abandoned baby, but they didn't know who she was. My family never mentioned to anyone that Lulu was adopted by my uncle and aunt. When the neighbors saw that my skin looked so different from that of any other child in the family and that I had just returned from the countryside, they called me "Darkie." They said that I was picked up on the road because nobody wanted me.

Several times I confronted my mother with the rumors that I heard from the neighbors. Each time my mother would deny it and immediately change the subject to something else. However, the rumors never stopped. These words hurt me deeply, and I grew up with them. They became wounds and then scarred me inside after a long period of time, and no one ever asked or cared about what effect their comments had on me. Besides, I was never my mother's favorite child. I mistakenly thought I was an outcast and developed a great inferiority complex. As a result, I emerged with a warped mindset, and to get attention I became very naughty.

When my grandmother wasn't paying attention, I would climb up the mulberry tree in front of her house and hide myself. Then I would pick the unripe mulberries and either eat them or throw them onto the heads of passersby. The passerby would appeal to my grandmother, and my grandmother would wave a long bamboo pole, used for hanging clothes, and shout, "Hurry down, or I will break your legs, then see if you'll climb again!" She didn't allow me to climb the tree. She was afraid I would fall and hurt myself. Actually, that was the love from God through my grandmother. He wanted to reprimand me for being so rude and discourteous.

Once in elementary school, our teacher required students to gather grass after school for the rabbits that the school was raising. I didn't gather any grass but rather cut down a tree sapling that a farmer next to the school had worked very hard to cultivate. After being discovered by the farmer, I ran off with the bamboo basket for gathering grass still on my back. However, I was too young to run faster than an adult, and soon he caught me. The farmer almost slapped my face. He held me in custody and gave me a good scolding. It was not until the evening that he let me go home. When I reached home it was completely dark, and my parents beat me hard after learning the details. Later, I was forced to go back to the farmer and to apologize to him. Otherwise, I would have been punished more. At that time, I hated my parents and their discipline so much. I didn't understand why they would hurt me that much. Now I know why. They were the instruments that God used to discipline me. Because the Lord disciplines those he loves. (Heb. 12:6)

In early summer, the middle school let students out early. It was more than two hours before dinner, so I gathered some classmates to go to the Yangtze River and play in the water. In those days the river didn't have any muddy sand, and it was clear and bright. There were many small ponds by the river; little fish and tadpoles lived in almost every one of them. I led my friends to dig a big pond and collected all the little fish and tadpoles from each small pond. We put them into our pond and then watched them swim around. We played happily, forgot the time, and didn't go home until it was getting dark.

We often had water fights by the river. The summer in Chongqing was very hot so by the time I got home, my clothes and trousers would already have dried out. Each time before returning home I cleaned the sand from my legs carefully. However, my father was a smart man and could always detect the difference. He asked me where I had gone after school. I first said I hadn't gone anywhere, and then I lied saying that I had been helping clean up at school. My father asked me to stretch out one of my legs. Then he scratched my leg from the bottom up with his fingers. The skin showed the evidence of my having been in the river. By this method, I was caught many times and suffered beatings and scolding.

There was a reason for being scolded. When my father was a youngster, he was swept away one day by a wave while playing in the river, and he almost died. He didn't know how to swim at the time and just flopped about in the water. Luckily, an old man, who was enjoying the shade nearby, saw him struggling. The old man grabbed a bamboo pole, ran to him, and shouted to him. My father grabbed the other end of the pole and was fished out.

After that experience, my father was afraid of the river and stayed a long way from it. When he became a parent, he strictly forbade my sister and me to play in the river, but I was stubborn. I had a mind of my own and always went against his directions. The little fish and tadpoles were so interesting that they made me forget what my father had said, so I was disciplined many times. Each time after being punished, I hated my father for being mean and blamed him for not knowing how to love and care for me, but now, I am very grateful for the mercy of the Lord. Without God putting my father in my life, I would not become the person I am today.

I remember when spring came again, my uncle always made beautiful kites out of paper for Lulu. When Lulu was first adopted, my uncle and aunt had thought they would have their own child, yet it never happened. They poured all their love out on Lulu, their only child. When my uncle saw that Lulu loved the kites, he made some for her each year. I would borrow one of them and have so much fun watching the kite fly in the sky with its long tail. One day the kite fell to the ground, and the paper was torn. I tried to fix the broken part. Unfortunately, the harder I tried, the worse it became. I then tore off all the paper. I dared not face my uncle and Lulu with the frame only, so I threw away the frame and went home empty-handed. Lulu didn't get her beloved kite back. She appealed to my uncle in tears, and my uncle spoke with my father. Not only was I whipped, but I also had to apologize to Lulu until she forgave me. I was bitterly humiliated.

Looking back, I saw how God was trying to discipline me through all these people—my grandmother, the farmer, my uncle, and my father. God wanted me to learn some valuable lessons from each one of them, such as, to respect others, to cherish other's hard work and friendship, and to be honest, responsible and trustworthy. However, as a rebellious youngster, I didn't pay that much attention to those teachings, and I put myself in various dangerous situations.

Chapter 15

WHEN I WAS IN DANGER, HE PROTECTED ME

As time went on and as I grew older, I didn't restrain my naughty personality. Several times I found myself in life-threatening circumstances, but each time, the Lord Jesus protected me with His invisible hands and always brought me back safely.

There was a disabled boy living on the seventh floor of our building. When he was a young child he had had a high fever, and his family didn't have enough money for medical treatment. As a result, he suffered serious debilitating effects from polio. He was tall, his teeth were always showing, and saliva constantly ran out of his mouth. His hands were like claws, and they were bent over at about ninety degrees. He couldn't speak except to make "yi-yi, wa-wa" sounds. His feet were turned inward, and he walked very slowly.

I didn't have a merciful heart at the time. I loved to tease him and laugh at him. Frequently, I purposely angered him. Because of this, he was very unkind to me. Once, my beloved black cat didn't come home. Later, I found that he had locked my cat in his kitchen. I became very angry and I pushed him almost knocking him over. From then on, he hated me and looked at me with glaring eyes. He used every conceivable means to retaliate.

One day when I was passing by the building, something fell from the sky and landed a step away from me. It broke into pieces and really frightened me. I looked up but didn't see anyone near the balcony railings from the first to the seventh floor. How could a brick drop from the sky by itself? I didn't believe there were any ghosts. Someone did it. I ran up to the seventh floor without stopping and caught the disabled boy while he was fleeing. I punched him angrily with no mercy. Then I raced home and locked the door tightly.

The disabled boy didn't appeal to my parents, and I was fine. Perhaps he knew he was the one who was at fault, but it scared me to even think about it. If that brick had fallen on my head, wouldn't it have cracked my head open and killed me? If so, I would not have been able to go to school again. Although I was not a good student at school, I didn't want to die. I decided it would be better for me to not offend others in the future. Looking back on that day, I believed that it was the grace of Jesus that saved me from that falling brick.

I remember a time when I was ill. One day before my mother left home, she handed a small bag with all my medications in it to my father and told him which pills I needed to take and what times I should take them. When the time came, my father called me and gave me the medicine bag. He told me what to do while reading his magazine at the same time. He trusted me because he thought I was old enough to understand and follow his instructions.

A little while later, my father finished reading and came to ask me, "Where are the remaining pills?"

"There is nothing left; I took them all, as you told me," I answered.

My father panicked, and his face suddenly changed. He screamed at me, "I only told you to take one-third of them. How could you take them all? Don't you know an overdose could kill you?"

I felt so foolish. Why didn't I listen to my father? In fact, I never really listened to him. I always thought about something else when he talked to me.

My mother came home early to cook for some guests who were coming for dinner. I started to feel dizzy so my mother called my grandmother, since she was older and had more life experience. My family was poor and had no money to send me to the hospital. Perhaps my grandmother had some old remedy to save my life. My grandmother immediately made a big bowl of soup mixed with green beans and ginger. I drank it and then lay on the bed without moving an inch. My grandmother and my mother came to check on me every half hour to see if I was still breathing. Later that night, I was fine and the next day I was back to normal. My mother said I had been lucky. The way I see it, it was the protection of Jesus that kept me from dying.

During my third year in high school, I lived at school. In those days, the school food court was really not hygienic. Food was left uncovered and at the mercy of flies and mosquitoes. One day, after eating dirty food, I suffered food poisoning, and I spent two weeks in the hospital. That was right before the college entrance exam, and I had to make time to study. I went back to school before I completely recovered. My school was located on the top of a hill in a different town and was far away from my home. It took more than one hour by boat, and then about forty-five minutes of quick walking uphill. On both sides of the road were farmer's fields, and almost no one lived there. Generally speaking, no one walked there after sundown, especially females.

When I returned to school, I left home late that day. I had a school bag on my shoulder and was walking along the road alone at about twilight. While I was walking, I felt like someone was following me. The footsteps behind me made the sound "sha sha sha". They sounded as if they were about 100 meters or so in back of me. If I walked faster, the sound of the stranger's footsteps increased in speed. If I slowed down, the footsteps slowed down also. Something was terribly wrong! I turned my head back while I was walking and saw a man following me stealthily, only two hundred meters away. Realizing I had seen him, he made no attempt to conceal himself anymore, and started to run fast toward me. I was scared and started to run too. I couldn't believe how weak I was from the sickness. My legs were shaky, and soon after I started to run, I was out of breath. The stalker kept chasing me, coming closer and closer.

Night had fallen, everything around me had become blurred. I had just reached a turn in the road. There was a wood on the left side and an abrupt slope on the right with rough grass and low bushes down the slope. If the stalker caught me and pushed me down the slope, I would be finished. I was so frightened that I didn't know what to do. The worse thing was that I heard other men's voices out of the darkness coming towards me at this moment. I thought that they belonged to the same group as the stalker who was chasing me. I thought, *What can I do? I am right in the middle of this group of bad guys. How can I possibly get away?* I was totally horrified, and my legs could no longer move. I stopped, trembled, and waited to be seized.

The strange thing was that the voices coming toward me stopped right in front of me. I peered forward and saw that two of my teachers were on their way home. One was my PE teacher who was in great shape. They saw I looked panic-stricken and asked why. My tongue moved around in my mouth, and I stuttered, "Someone is chasing after me." Then I couldn't say anything more but could only move my hands randomly. The teachers were smart enough to understand what was happening. They told me to stand there and not be afraid.

"I want to see who's got the guts to prowl around here!" The PE teacher shouted after the pursuer. Just at that moment, a truck drove by. Seeing a few people standing in the middle of the road, the driver slowed down. The pursuer saw that the one person he was stalking had become three. He became even more terrified than I. He jumped up, grabbed the door handle of the truck, and rode away on the truck.

My teachers were very kind. They were worried that I was walking outside at night, so they accompanied me back to school and chatted with me on the way. "Our original plan was to go home in the afternoon," they said, "but then something came up at the last minute. So we changed our plans, stayed at school, and didn't set out until after dinner. We didn't expect to see you here, but fortunately we did. Otherwise the outcome could have been serious." They urged me again and again, "A feeble girl like you should never be out walking alone at nightfall, especially on a hilly road. The world we live in isn't safe. Bad men still exist, and things like killing for money sometimes do happen. Please be careful!"

I never forgot this alarming episode. The Lord knew what was going to happen, so He had the teachers alter their plans and delay going home. If it wasn't for the Lord sending these two teachers along to protect me at that dangerous moment, how could I have gotten away from the stalker's hands? Of course I couldn't have!

I used to consider these kinds of events merely as coincidence. Now I believe that nothing is a coincidence; there never are any coincidences! The reason that the brick didn't hit my head, the overdose didn't kill me, and the stalker didn't succeed in catching me, was because the Holy Spirit of God guarded me unceasingly day and night. It was Jesus who gave me chance after chance and brought me back from within an inch of death each time. He hoped that I would recognize His existence from those experiences, but I refused to come to my senses until a greater crisis destroyed my marriage.

Chapter 16

WHEN I WAS BROKEN,
HE RESTORED ME

After I graduated from High school, I met my future husband through a friend of mine. He was a guy of few words working as a mechanic for a public transportation company. From what I saw, he seemed to be a very responsible and caring person. After dating for nine months, I felt that he was the one that I could trust and spend the rest of my life with. I decided to marry him. We got married in the Summer of 1992.

Soon after marriage, my husband went back to his old habits: smoking, drinking, and gambling on Ma-Jiang. All of the promises that he had made before our marriage became just empty words. He tried to persuade me to gamble as well, but I preferred reading books or studying English. He often jeered at me, saying, "Everyone is gambling on Ma-Jiang except you. You're a social drop out. Why do you study English? What's the use of learning it in such a small town? Will you go abroad?"

When I was pregnant, he was out a lot, often staying away for several nights at a time. The reasons he gave were always the same. They always had to do with his work, which was repairing buses when they were broken down on the road. He would tell me that he was too busy to call me. I expected him to return home on time but was often disappointed. Sometimes he would come home a few days later, and silence was his only explanation. He would say to me, "Don't ask too much. As a woman, you should be satisfied if I have money to bring home." I felt disrespected by the way he treated me. For this reason, we had frequent arguments.

The night my water broke I could not find him, and my parents accompanied me to the hospital. The doctor requested a signature from my husband prior to admission and asked where he was. I said I didn't know. The doctor looked at me and said, "What kind of man is this? His wife is ready to give birth, and she doesn't even know where he is. A normal man would have asked for leave and be waiting at the hospital." I felt awful and wanted to cry, but I swallowed my tears because the marriage was my own choice. Whom else could I blame?

In May 1993 my baby girl was born, and she looked exactly like her father. The eyes, nose, eyebrows and even the hair looked like his. Unfortunately, there were no smiles on my husband's face. He showed up at the hospital three days later, but after that he disappeared again. When I was discharged from the hospital on the seventh day, my parents hired a pedicab to take me to their home to recuperate. They were so upset at my husband's attitude and behavior. One day when he appeared, my mother urged him to be kind to me and to the newborn baby, but he turned a deaf ear to her. He used dirty language in a big argument with my mother. He slammed the door and then left.

I thought it was only an impulsive act and that he had left in a fit of anger. Even if he didn't want to see my mother, he should at least want to see me and his baby. Three days went by, but he didn't show up. Seven days went by, and he still didn't show up. I waited every day and every moment. Any sound outside the door made me think he was coming home. I hoped to hear his footsteps approaching and to hear a knock at the door. I expected he would appear with flowers in his hands, with a smile on his face and with a tender expression. I wished he would hold our baby girl, kiss her, and tell me how beautiful and cute she was.

However, the sun rose and set. Two weeks passed. My birthday passed. Our baby girl had grown a whole month, and he still didn't appear. Forty days later there was still no sign of him. I was worried about him all the time. Was he still alive or not? Why hadn't he come home yet? I never thought that he would abandon us like this. My marriage was collapsing because of endless worry about my husband and disappointment in his lack of love and care for me and our baby. My emotions were a total mess.

While I was growing up, I had always thought of myself as the adopted child of my family. It was not until I was twenty years old when my mother finally clarified the confusion surrounding my birth, but the damage was done. For twenty years I was never my mother's favorite child. I had been deeply hurt, and had many quarrels with my mother. Our relationship grew cold. I thought my parents didn't love me at all. I wanted to get out of the house, a place I disliked so much, and start a new life for my own happiness and freedom. I got married without really thinking or examining carefully who this man was. My parents had told me that he was unsuitable for me. I didn't listen to them, but married him without their blessings.

Unfortunately, my husband did not care for me in my time of need. At this time my parents stepped forward and helped my baby and me. They took my daughter and me into their home and carefully looked after us. I felt their love. It was during this time, I realized that what I had thought about my parents was wrong. They did love me. If there hadn't been love, my newborn baby and I wouldn't have ended up staying in such a warm and comfortable home. If there hadn't been love, my parents wouldn't have provided me with daily meals and washed my baby's clothes and diapers after a busy working day. My heart was filled with appreciation for them and guilt for my behavior all at the same time. This experience changed my perspective and attitude toward my parents.

Then I understood the meaning of "parents are always parents." They are the ones who loved me the most. Blood is thicker than water, and their love would never be cut off from me. Looking back, my strict upbringing had been good for me. Although there had been many beatings, they trained me to walk the right path. No matter how angry, disappointed, or worried my parents were, they had forgiven and accepted me. They had taken care of me and protected me. This was love. Their love made me reflect and regret past decisions, and it cleared away the barriers between my parents and me. Thankfully, our relationship changed for the better.

I wanted to pass on this love to my daughter, but when I saw my infant baby, who had just come into this world and had been snubbed by her own father, I was heartbroken. Day after day I cried when no one else was around. When others had babies, whether a boy or a girl, they would celebrate with the whole family. I thought, *What about me?* I didn't even know where my husband was. I knew in some men's minds that boys are preferred to carry on the family line, but I was not able to choose whether it would be a boy or a girl. Everyone said that a child could strongly bond a marriage, but it was the destruction of mine. However, that was neither my fault nor my daughter's.

My husband's abandonment and coldness deeply hurt me. I would often feel my heart bleeding as if a sharp knife had pierced it. No one could understand that kind of pain. Gradually, I started to hate him. I hated his face and everything about him. If I had had a gun with a bullet in it, I would have used it. If I had been stronger than him, I would have used a pair of scissors and plunged them into his chest. This hatefulness swallowed my happiness. It made me lose my patience and hope, and I was on the verge of a mental collapse.

I could not understand why some people were willing to adopt orphans, love them, and take care of them, but the father of my child would not do anything for his own daughter. I remembered seeing movies in which people would kneel down and cry out to heaven in their desperation saying, "God, forgive me!" I thought to myself, *Does God really exist? Does He have power over human beings? Is this a punishment I'm receiving from God because I have never believed in His existence and have blasphemed Him?* I was very confused.

Looking at the ceiling I started to cry out, "God, if you really exist, please let me have a good night's sleep. I've lived in constant apprehension and haven't had a good night's rest since my husband left. I've become so anxious thinking about him day and night. I'm worried that he's hungry and tired, or doesn't eat or sleep well outside, and is bullied by others, since he's a man of few words. I'm exhausted now. I do not want to think about him anymore. I need sleep, if only one night or even for just a couple of hours."

I promised myself on that day, "If I sleep well tonight, I will believe that there is a God, and I will follow Him for the rest of my life." That was the first time that I talked to God. Even though I didn't know whether He really existed, I was serious. What surprised me was that I had a very deep and peaceful sleep that night. All the fears of being abandoned while pregnant disappeared. The next morning, when I woke up, I said, "God, it seems like you really are there. Thank you for giving me a good night's sleep. Thank you for giving me peace."

After my recuperation I continued to stay at my parents' house. My husband didn't accept my request for a divorce. He threatened me and said that he would rather go to jail than get a divorce. At that time, two murders occurred in our little town, because two women had requested a divorce from their husbands. In both cases, the husbands had killed their wives and seriously injured the rest of the wife's family. What I heard from my husband made me so frightened that I became desperate for my family and my future. My parents were also worried and warned me to be very careful. They advised me not to leave him unless I had a very good reason.

Having no other choice, I talked to God again, "God, if you really exist, please take me out of this town and never bring me back. My heart has been broken. My memories are awful. I want to get away from this place as far as I can." One more time I promised God, if that day came, I would believe in His existence and follow Him for the rest of my life.

After that, I forgot my request and promise that I had made and continued to live as an atheist. However, God didn't forget. He remembered very well. Soon He gave me a chance to leave my hometown and also my estranged husband. The department where I worked provided an opportunity for continuing education and training. In September of 1994, I left my one year old daughter with my parents and went to Chengdu University of Traditional Chinese Medicine, which was about three hundred miles away from my home.

The day I left I carried only a little luggage. With bitterness and grief from a broken heart and with endless love toward my daughter, I stepped onto the boat. When the whistle on the boat blew, I looked back to the riverbank and said goodbye to my hometown. Tears filled my eyes. I asked myself, *What have I done wrong? Why do I have to be uprooted to a place I don't even know? Why is it me leaving this land rather than my husband?* Not knowing the future that was waiting for me, I decided to continue on this path and never go back.

The boat under my feet was sailing upriver. Although it was moving very slowly, it had already left the dock and eventually it would reach its destination and its resting place. I thought to myself, *But where is my destiny? Where is my resting place? When those people get out of the boat, they will go to a place where they belong and be welcomed and loved by their love ones. But where do I belong? Where is my love? Is there any true love in this world? If there is, how can I find it?* I had no answers for any of these questions. All I could do was to bury them in my heart.

Leaving my daughter with my parents and moving to Chengdu was the most painful and desperate moment of my life. I didn't expect that it would also be the moment that I was led into the God's path of truth. Through those pains and desperations, weakness and wonders, God would gradually lead me toward His throne so that I could experience His true love, which was constant and unconditional. He accompanied me to the end of my old life and also to the beginning of a new life.

After my first year studying in Chengdu, I finally divorced my husband in 1995. My parents were taking care of my daughter in our hometown, so I had no burdens in my daily life and had nothing to worry about. I started to have the freedom again that all young people enjoy. However, while I had regained my freedom, I found that I had lost my passion for life, my sense of security, and my trust in other people. The results of the divorce were grief, hate, loneliness, and emptiness, which were indescribable.

I thought I was a good woman and I tried to live a moral life. I was loyal to my husband and I never had the habits of smoking or drinking or gambling. I kept myself away from cheating or stealing. I thought if I didn't do those things I would have a happy life. However, I was betrayed in the midst of my good efforts to be faithful. The time came when I was forced to deal with these terrible emotions and feelings that came as a result of my pain from my divorce. I felt that life was very unfair, and I didn't understand why I had to suffer so much.

I was still young with a beautiful face, smooth skin, shining eyes, an enchanting smile, and a lovely figure. I didn't need to go out looking for men; men chased after me. I started to date new boyfriends and soon I lost my way in the metropolis. I found that no one could make me feel warm inside and I could not trust any of them, because their desires did not match what I wanted. I was so empty and lonely that I often asked myself, *What is life all about? If this is life, I'd rather not have it.*

I didn't want to go anywhere when any holidays came. I didn't want the sympathy of others, and I didn't want to be seen crying by others. I had to be strong for my daughter. When no one else was around me, I pined more and more for the ocean, the paradise of my dreams. I was sad, but I thought that happiness was there. I was troubled, but joy was there. I was fretting, but peace was there. I was disappointed, but hope was there. My heart was locked, but the ocean was wide open.

Before I married, I was very romantic and had had many desires and dreams. I had desired to have a true love and to be loved truly. I had desired a soul mate and a lifetime companion. I had dreamed of never forsaking or being forsaken. I had dreamed of holding hands and being held forever; however, everything had become futile, and the only thing left in those long lonely nights was to imagine seeing the ocean and letting my dreams fly with the seagulls.

I could hide myself from others, but not from the Lord Jesus. He knew my desires and dreams. He saw the tears in my eyes and the bitterness in my tears. He saw the wounds in my heart and the pain in the wounds. He saw I lived miserably in my sins, and He knew I could no longer bear such a heavy burden. He didn't want me to remain in my confusion. He wanted to set me free and lead me to the right path. And He knew that only the truth could set me free.

When I began my Sanya journey in 1996, Jesus was with me. He held my hand quietly and flew with me over the mountains, the plains, and the seas. He went with me to the paradise of my dreams. There, through the emotions expressed from His indescribable eyes, the nail wounds in His hands, and the blood that poured forth from His heart, He generously showed me the true love and companionship that I had been longing for. He shifted my focus away from myself onto Him.

I felt humiliated by the way I had been treated in my marriage, and I thought I was the most hurt person in the world. Jesus didn't do anything wrong, yet He was crucified on the cross. The people around him laughed at Him and flogged Him. They insulted Him and spat on His face. People put a crown of thorns on His head and watched the blood flowing down from His brow. In fact, Jesus was the most hurt person in the world.

When I recalled my vision in which the bleeding Jesus was standing right before me, I realized how selfish and narrow-minded I was, and how unselfish and broad-minded He was. Only one person in this world had hurt me: my husband. Yet all the people of this world had hurt Jesus. After I was abandoned I felt like my heart had a hole in it and that blood was dripping out of it, yet in my vision Jesus' heart did have a hole in it from which poured out His living blood. The pain I had experienced, although overwhelming at times for me, was not as great as the pain Jesus experienced when He suffered for all humanity. The pain Jesus had was beyond what anyone could ever imagine.

I could never talk about my divorce with anyone because the memory was so painful and I couldn't face it. I buried my grief deep in my heart along with my bitterness, disappointment, hatred, and anger. I promised myself that I would never forgive the person who had hurt me so deeply, yet I also had hurt Jesus just as deeply by not acknowledging Him. In fact, I was totally worthy of being judged by Him. However, He didn't blame me but rather said, "My child, you have come back at last. I have been waiting for you for so long!" When He was crucified on the cross and bore all the faults of the world, He didn't choose to hate all the people who had wronged Him, but rather to lavish them with His love, mercy and forgiveness. He opened His arms wide and said, "Father, forgive them, for they do not know what they are doing." (Luke 23:34) How great is His forgiveness!

Although I had waited for the father of my daughter from morning to evening, sunrise to sunset, dawn to dusk, I had done so for only forty days. When he had not come, I had shut the door in my heart and didn't want to see him anymore, but Jesus had waited much longer for me. He had waited until flowers blossomed, ice melted, leaves fell, geese migrated. Day after day, year after year, spring to autumn, and summer to winter. He had waited for many years. And He was still waiting. Meanwhile, He forgave all my sins and gave me more opportunities. He was waiting for the day that I would finally return to Him.

The love and the mercy of Christ opened my mind and set me free from the tomb of selfishness. His true light exposed the hatred and anger in my heart. I saw the bitterness and corruption in me; nevertheless, I could not deny His unconditional and constant love for me. I started to think, *How many people in the world are experiencing what I have experienced and have a miserable life? How many people are burdened with hatred as I am? How many people are living in the tomb that I used to live in and are living like they are already dead? Why can't I reach out my hands to brothers and sisters who are suffering? Why can't I help them through the darkest moments of their journey?*

Jesus made me understand the real meaning of life. It is not being immersed in the past but facing the future. It is not enumerating our sufferings but counting the grace of Christ. It means not collecting the tears of sorrow, but rather cherishing the lessons that He teaches us. It is not waiting to receive love or hoping for it to be returned, but rather giving it out without expecting to be paid back, just like Jesus Himself did. Freely He gave us love, so we should freely share our love with others, for it is more blessed to give than to receive. (Acts 20:35)

Eventually, after looking at my past life and comparing my love to God's love, I forgave the father of my daughter from the bottom of my heart. All my anger and hatred for him over the years gradually disappeared. Ever since then, I have felt comfortable and cozy as if the sun was shining upon me. I had peace and joy again that no one in the world could give or take away from me. I felt blessed and satisfied.

How I thank Jesus. When I was completely broken, He restored me. It was He who set me free from the bondage of hatred. It was His injuries that healed my pain. It was His crucifixion that repaired my brokenness. It was He who shifted the burden from my shoulders onto His, so that I could hold my head high and live like a new person. His grace really is vast and countless. Who says life cannot start over again? In the love of Jesus, nothing is impossible. Everything can be renewed, and every day is a new beginning.

Chapter 17

SOMETHING BETTER IS COMING

*A*fter my baptism in 1999 I began to dream about my future marriage again. I thought, *Perhaps God will bring me a man to be my husband, and that man will take me to a beautiful place that I have never been to. My daughter could join us, and we could have a new life in that place.* However, whom I should choose to marry was a big headache for me.

When I was in Chengdu University of Traditional Chinese Medicine, there was a young man who was pursuing me. He chased after me for two years and had wanted to marry me. I liked him a lot but I could not make up my mind. In 1996 after my Sanya journey, I decided to accept this young man's offer and build a family with him. I went to visit him and his family in a small town in Xinjiang Provence with a sincere desire to start a new life with this young man.

Before his family knew I was a divorced woman, they loved me and treated me well. However, everything changed from the moment they learned the truth about my past. In those days in China, a divorced woman with a child, especially with a girl, was discriminated against. His parents wanted to stop the marriage. His mother said to me, "If you really want to marry my son, that's fine, but you are not allowed to bring your daughter along with you. Our family has a good reputation in this town. My son has never married, but you have been divorced. You already have a daughter and will want to bring her with you when you get married to my son. This would really ruin our family's reputation." My boyfriend had to choose between his mother's wish or mine; he chose to obey his mother.

In order to marry him, I would have to leave my daughter behind. Facing this choice, I knew that I could abandon everything *except* my daughter. I couldn't pursue my own happiness and leave her faraway in my hometown with my parents, for I would be worrying about her all the time. I had experienced rejection and hurt when I was little, and I didn't want my daughter to have the same experience. I thought to myself, *If marriage was going to start in such a painful condition, how could I possibly find joy or happiness or hope in it? What's wrong with divorce? Must I live an inferior life because of this?*

In that town, I had no relatives. I only had the God I had seen in my vision. I felt I needed to talk to someone who knew God before I left the town. I found a shabby church in the suburbs that was managed by an elder, who was over fifty years old, and his father, who was in his seventies. They were from Henan Province. Three generations of the family had sold their assets and come to minister to the people in that area. At that time, the elder was the only one there; his father was out visiting a parishioner.

After a short chat the old man brought me into the sanctuary where I saw two large banners made with white paper pinned on the cracked wall. The banners faced the entrance of the sanctuary, so it was the first thing people saw when they came into this place. One banner said, "God so loved the world" and the other said, "God is love". These banners reminded me of my experience in Sanya and my experience of God's love for me. The young man's family rejected me because I was a divorced woman with a daughter. I had no value in their eyes, yet God had never rejected me. He accepted me and embraced me as a filthy sinner. He cherished me as someone would cherish a diamond, and He loved me unconditionally! I felt I had come to the right place and found the right person to talk to.

After visiting the sanctuary, the old man brought me back to the place where we were before. He said, "Come in and have a seat, sister. It's cold outside." He led me to a room serving as both his office and bedroom. After some hesitation, I entered the room. It was so small that I quickly saw everything in it. I couldn't believe their austere life. They had two benches, two tables, two cups, two quilts and two beds. It reminded me of when I was living in a simple apartment in Chengdu. I felt great respect for him, and ashamed of myself because I hadn't chosen to give up everything to follow the

Lord. In the sea in Sanya, the glorious God had revealed Himself to me. His true light had illuminated me, and His love and mercy had embraced me. I thought to myself, *How many people in the world have had experiences like me? Why didn't I have the courage to lay down everything and live for God, just like this old man and his father did?* I wondered how many people in the world were quietly dedicating their lives to God like them.

Noticing my worried frown, the old man asked, "Why did you come here, sister?" Nervous and uneasy, I told him my situation, the choice that I had to make, and my uncertainty about my future. "Go back," he said, "it's the right thing to do. God has closed this door for you. He will certainly lead you and open another one for you. Just go back to Chengdu. We will surely pray for you." The eyes of the old man revealed fatherly care and affection, which really comforted me and calmed my heart.

While I was still there, the first snow fell on the small town. My heart, however, had already experienced winter much earlier than the town did. With great disappointment I left Xinjiang. When the train roared through the open field, I could not help but shed tears. I had thought that this young man truly loved me. I had dreamed that happiness would welcome me with open arms, and that I wouldn't need to drift anymore, but everything I had dreamed turned out to be bubbles that evaporated instantly. *Goodbye, my dream, good-bye, I will never return to this place again.* I decided that I would just let this beautiful yet unreal love story remain in that cold land forever. I tore all his letters and photos to pieces, and I opened my hands and let them blow away with the wind.

It was a three-day and three-night journey from that town in Xinjiang back to Chengdu where I had been living and working. I climbed to the upper berth and cried for one day and one night. My life was over, and there was no hope anymore. If this family didn't accept my daughter, other Chinese families wouldn't either, and I would never get married again. I thought to myself, *But what's wrong with having a daughter? She is pretty and smart. Why wouldn't his family accept her? Why didn't they even want to meet her?* The train thundered down the track as I wept bitterly. I felt brokenhearted again, for my daughter and for myself.

I don't know how long I cried before I fell asleep. Suddenly, a magnificent, rich voice whispered in my ear, "Something better is coming! Something better is coming!" The sentence was repeated twice and was very clear. The voice was steady, thunderous, and awesome. It had absolute authority. At that moment, all I could hear was the voice. The roar of the train wheels had faded away.

What a familiar voice! I had heard it somewhere before. I immediately turned over and sat up to see who was talking to me, but I did not see anyone around, and I didn't know where the rest of the people in the train could have gone. "Where have I heard this voice before?" I asked myself again. All of a sudden it came to me that in the sea of Sanya God had spoken to me in just such a voice, "My child, you have come back at last. I have been waiting for you for so long." And God had said, "Go, help her" with the same voice.

I thought, *Oh, God is talking to me again. He has a promise for me*. Instantly, I was greatly comforted. The worried furrows on my forehead smoothed, and a smile came across my face. I was over-joyed. What is more precious and credible than a promise from God? I remembered that old man. He must have kept his promise and prayed for me. Even though I didn't know what prayer was at that time, based on what I heard, I firmly believed that God must have prepared a bright future for me.

Because of this horrible experience in Xinjiang, I decided to not marry a Chinese man. I would wait for someone from another country who would accept my daughter and me. I didn't know how that would happen. So I cried out to the Lord and asked for His help. I thought that day would never arrive. To my great surprise, a life-changing opportunity did come four years later after my trip to Xinjiang.

At the end of March in the year 2000 while I was serving as an interpreter for foreign students at the Chengdu University of Traditional Chinese Medicine, a team of Americans came to learn Chinese acupuncture. Three-and-half weeks after they had arrived, Graham, a tall handsome American man, who was originally from England, proposed to me and invited me to visit the United States. This marriage proposal was totally unexpected. I had only interpreted for him once. I wasn't familiar with him at all, and I had no relatives or friends in the United States. As a result, I refused his offer, but he implored me, "Just consider it a free vacation to the United States. You can return home if you don't like it, and you won't lose anything." Thinking this was quite reasonable, I agreed to his suggestion but with one condition: I was not going to cohabit with him during my stay.

My decision greatly pleased Graham. He immediately went with me to my home town to help me apply for a passport. In order to honor my parents, he invited them for tea at the hotel where he was staying. My father went alone. Graham explained his reason for inviting me to the United States. He told my father to not worry about anything because he was going to take care of all my needs during my stay, and he assured my father that I would return home safely. By the time my father walked out of the hotel, he encouraged me to go in order to explore a chance for a new life. My parents promised me that they would take good care of my daughter while I was away.

While I was waiting for the arrival of my passport, Graham's study program in Chengdu was over, and he left China to return to San Francisco where he lived. He kept telephoning and emailing me every day. A few months later, I received a package from him along with an international airline ticket that allowed me to fly from Chengdu to Shanghai, and then from Shanghai to San Francisco.

On September 13, 2000, I arrived in San Francisco, California. Graham took me to one of his Chinese friend's house to stay. This Chinese couple originally came from Chengdu. They welcomed and hosted me warmheartedly for a while. Then I stayed with another nice family who came originally from Hong Kong until I moved to a rented room provided by a wonderful old American couple, Ruth and Asher.

This old couple never treated me like a foreigner. They treated me like one of their own family members, and they required the rest of their family to do the same. They gave me new clothes and new shoes and took me to birthday parties. They drove me to different parks. They cooked me some food that I had never tasted before and occasionally brought me to restaurants to explore more American food. In addition, the man of the house even gave me a free English lesson each week. They gave me so much of their love, yet they never expected anything in return. They had made me feel that I was the luckiest person in the world.

During my stay, Graham helped me extend my visa through a legal immigration office. We spent more time together. We worshiped the Lord with other brothers and sisters from his church, walked along Pacifica State Beach, hiked Mount Diablo, took his friends' child to the Monterey Aquarium. We made day trips up and down the coast, enjoyed spending time on the Golden Gate Bridge. In July 2001 we got married in St. Stephen's Episcopal Church in Orinda, which is on the other side of San Francisco.

The night before the big day, Ruth and Asher handed me my wedding gift. It was an envelope that contained all my rent payments made by Graham. They told me in tears how much they loved me, enjoyed spending time with me, and how much they were going to miss me. The next day, they came to my wedding as my American family. After the wedding, Graham and I moved from San Francisco to Los Angeles, the best place to live, according to my husband. In 2002, we brought Wei Wei, my daughter, to San Marino, a small city of Los Angeles County, where we were living. My daughter and I were finally reunited in Los Angeles after many years of separation. In Los Angeles, this rich and beautiful land, we started a new chapter in the journey of life on the other side of the globe, far away from China.

Soon after my daughter came to live with my husband and me I found that my husband truly loved my daughter as his own. He took Wei Wei around to see his friends and introduced her by saying, "This is my daughter. Look at her nose and ears. Don't you think she looks just like me?" He washed her dirty clothes and shoes and spent countless hours helping her with her homework. He biked with her and taught her how to swim, encouraged her to make new friends and supported her to travel with them. He never missed any of her school events, and he always brought beautiful flowers along with his best wishes to WeiWei on her birthday.

Not only that, but Graham's family in England also extended their love toward Wei Wei by visiting us in Los Angeles, caring about each stage of her growth and sending her birthday cards, gifts and best wishes. Because of their love, Wei Wei's life had been transformed from being rejected and hurt by her biological father to being accepted and cared for by her new family outside of China.

Many times I thought of the old man who I had met in the church in Xinjiang. He was right. When God closes one door, He definitely opens another. Inside the door that God opened for me, I experienced countless blessings and grace. Many times when I savor my life and what the Lord had said to me on that train while I was leaving Xinjiang, I can't stop praising Jesus. He truly is the Lord of faithfulness who keeps His promises. Who else could I trust and rely on except Jesus, my Savior and my Lord?

Chapter 18

NOTHING IS IMPOSSIBLE FOR HIM

*I*n the first few years of my life in the United States, there wasn't any financial pressure on me, and I didn't need to work. Life was easy and comfortable, but my heart pursued the Lord less and less. Unexpectedly, my husband lost his job when the recession hit. We looked for shortcuts to make money and hired a real estate coach through a well-known national company to teach us how to make money fast. Very soon, the coach had persuaded us to go into joint real estate ventures with him. We would provide the funds and he would provide the expertise, and we would split the profits equally. Unfortunately, six months later, we found out that it was a fraudulent scheme. Not only did we lose more money, but we also had to hire two lawyers to deal with the case because the business was located in different states.

At the same time our business with another friend also lost large sums because real estate values went down. An old English woman borrowed some money from us; three months later, we received a letter from a lawyer announcing that the woman was bankrupt. The money we had lent her wasn't a big sum, but it was still a significant loss. All of those failures came one after another without giving us a chance to breathe. Seeing our savings rapidly disappear within a short time, my husband didn't know what to do. I understood his frustration and wanted to get a job in order to generate income and reduce some of his pressure, but I didn't know how.

I had never really worked since I had come to America. My health was a big problem. I had been weak since my daughter was born. I often had headaches, sore throats, stomach aches, and back pain that never quit. Dizziness and vertigo accompanied me daily. I felt cold all over and tired all the time. I could not leave the doors or windows open for I was afraid of wind and drafts. I avoided every windy place, cold temperatures, and air-conditioning, because they would make the symptoms worse. Wherever I went and no matter how hot it was, I wore a hat, a scarf, a wind breaker, a shawl, and many layers of clothes. I looked so peculiar even my daughter was embarrassed to go out with me.

I frequently visited doctors, cooked herbal tea, and hoped to get better every day. No matter how much I did, my illness became worse and worse. How was I to get by living in America? Where was the hope? I didn't know. I earnestly prayed daily, talking with the Lord, and hoping that He would send someone to guide me in the right direction. However, there was no answer to my prayers, and no one came. Facing the future, I was frightened, desperate, and helpless. I often cried quietly to myself.

I started to complain more and more. "Lord Jesus, you promised to lead me to a place with milk and honey, but now, after almost one year my husband still cannot find a job. We have no income, my daughter is in high school, and there are many expenses. Did you bring me here to become broke and live in poverty? I have being waiting to regain my health so that I can witness for you. But even in the summertime, I have had to wear winter clothes and a hat, see doctors, and continuously take herbal tea. If things continue like this, who will believe that you are the Almighty God, the miracle God, and the healing God?"

Just when I was totally disappointed, I received a letter from a couple in Shanghai. I had met them at the Shanghai International Church before coming to the United States, but we had never contacted each other by mail. There was a piece of paper in the letter, a testimony that could make anyone cry. It spoke of a boy named Yang who was abandoned by his parents and made an orphan. He was later adopted. However, he was disobedient, illiterate and useless. He had left home, joined gangs, became the leader of a gang, and stole from many places.

One time, Young's gang was chased by police after fighting with another gang which resulted in injuries to that other gang. Yang's gang ran into the primitive forest of the Great Xingan Mountains and hid in a cave. An unexpected heavy snow fell that night, and the temperature suddenly dropped to thirty degrees below zero centigrade. When rescuers arrived the next day, nine out of thirteen gang members were dead, and the remaining four were disabled.

After waking up in the hospital, Yang had found that his lower legs and hands had been cut off. Feeling desperate, he had crawled to a window in the hospital hallway on the third floor and threw himself out when no one was watching him. However, he fell into a construction security net that had been set outside the second floor, and he was unharmed. After getting out of the hospital, he started begging, but he continued to command his gang members secretly. They did atrocious things everywhere.

One day, when Yang was being chased by police, he crawled into a church to hide, where he received a warm reception, and so he stayed there overnight. He woke in the middle of the night and heard a voice praying for him. Opening his eyes, he saw a cross, and all the sins of his life were replayed before him. Immediately, he repented in tears and became a disciple. Later, brothers and sisters in Christ donated some money and fitted Yang with artificial legs. He then traveled widely, witnessing for the Lord Jesus.

I couldn't help weeping profusely as soon as I read this story. Something like an electric current went over my body, and I could not stand up. It was the touch of the Holy Spirit. Leaning against the wall, I was able to walk to the sofa. With both legs trembling, I sat down.

How similar my experience had been to that of brother Yang's! This was nothing else, but the power from the same Lord. I was deeply touched by the love of Christ as I read this story.

We were both prodigals, sinful and unpardonable. One was escaping from the police; the other was avoiding being hunted by the devil. One crawled on the ground; the other swam in the sea. One slept in a church; the other struggled in the ocean. One heard a voice praying for him; the other didn't even know someone was quietly praying for her. One saw the cross and all of his past sins appeared before him; the other saw Jesus and all of her past sins appeared in front of her. Both broke down in tears, confessed their sins, and repented. Both were forgiven by the grace of Jesus. Both were redeemed, and both became disciples of the Lord.

The only difference was that brother Yang became a witness for Christ after he was saved, yet I could not even walk out of my home due to my illness. I thanked God that He had never forgotten me. He reminded me again through Yang's testimony that He is the only way and that I could regain my health by looking upon Him. Once more, Jesus had declared to me that only He was the Almighty God, the living God, the only true God, and the One that I should have faith in and look to.

Then I understood that my sickness wasn't physical but rather an ailment of a disobedient soul. I was the only one who knew Jesus in my family. The rest were still blind and living in darkness, but I had hardly prayed for them. Any new sins on my part and the sins of my family burdened me and kept me in bondage. I decided to put my health into the hands of Jesus and stop seeing doctors and drinking herbal teas. I wanted to confess, repent, ask forgiveness sincerely and be healed. I totally believed that if the Lord could keep Yang alive at thirty degrees below zero centigrade, He could also allow me to see a full recovery.

Before dawn the next day, I took my Bible with me and drove to a hill close to Eaton Canyon outside of Pasadena. After finding a quiet place, I started to pray. I could only sit inside my car because I was so afraid of being cold. "Lord Jesus," I said, "I've come to seek your face and ask to be healed. You said, "If you have faith the size of a mustard seed, you can say to this mountain, 'Move from here to there' and it will move." (Matt. 17:20) Now my faith is about the size of a large potato as big as my fist. It's hundreds of times bigger or hundreds of thousands of times bigger than a mustard seed, but I don't want to move a mountain. I only want to be cured. Please answer my prayer." Nothing happened on that day. The Lord kept silent, and it seemed like He was ignoring me.

The next morning, I went to the same place. I would not give up until He answered. I lifted up the Bible and said to the Lord, "Jesus, you have said, 'Ask and it will be given to you; seek and you will find; knock and the door will be opened to you.'" (Matt. 7:7) Those are your words, and the Bible is our contract. It has your signature everywhere. Today I am here, to knock on your door and to seek your face. I did my part regarding the contract, and I beg you also to do your part."

Nothing happened, and I continued my prayer, "You have said your name is the great 'I Am'. As for me, I am weak, but you are strong. I am disappointed, but you are the hope. I am a sufferer, and you are the comforter. I am the patient, but you are the doctor. You have said you are the Almighty God and nothing for you is impossible. You make the blind see and the dumb speak. You make hunchbacks straighten and the lame walk. You cure all of them. Please show me a miracle and cure me too." I cried these words to the Lord, but I felt that the Lord looked at me, shook His head, turned His back, and left me. Nothing was changed on that day. I was so disappointed and said to the Lord when I left the canyon, "Lord, I will not give up until you answer my prayer. I will come up here every day until I get your answer."

On the third morning, when it was still dark, I parked my car at a higher place on the hill. Holding my face in my hands, I prayed even more earnestly. "Lord Jesus, I have faith in you. You have said you are the Son of the living God, and you have authority to forgive sins. Please also forgive my sins. I knew I was saved, but I hardly ever prayed for my family's salvation. Please forgive my sin of selfishness. When my life was easy and comfortable, I forgot about your grace and let myself become estranged from you. Please forgive my sin of ingratitude. When I had no financial pressure and had an abundant supply, I didn't share with others. Please forgive my sin of greed. When I saw homeless people and beggars on the street, I didn't reach out a helping hand. Please forgive my sin of merciless-ness. When failures and difficulties came upon me, I complained endlessly. Please forgive my sin of complaining.

"My family refuses you. They don't want to know you, and con-tinue to worship the Goddess of Mercy and the Buddha. Please for-give their sins of not wanting to know you. Among them some may have committed adultery, stole, cheated, acted arrogantly, had out-bursts of anger, or blasphemed. Please pardon all their sins that they have committed and keep them from those sins that they haven't committed but might commit. Lord, forgive them all, for you have a merciful heart."

From my next of kin to my distant relatives, I recounted all the sins I could remember before the Lord. One-by-one, I presented them in front of His throne. I earnestly pleaded for myself and for my family. The more I pleaded, the more I realized that in this life Jesus Christ is our all in all. While I cried out to the Lord, I shed tears of remorse for the faults of my family and myself. The strange thing was that as soon as I confessed a sin, I felt something going out of my body, and my heavy heart gradually became lighter and lighter. It was as if a tight chain had been undone and pulled loose from around me.

I was tired after crying for so long, so I lay down in the back seat of my car and slept. Suddenly, I felt a warm current entering the soles of my feet and going to the upper part of my body, along the calf, up the back of the thigh, and straight along the lower back. "It is the hand of the Lord Jesus!" I sat up at once and exclaimed, "Jesus, you are here! Thank you for coming. Please continue to go up to those parts where I often feel cold and painful." I patted my shoulders, my upper arms, my neck, and my entire head with my hands. The warm current traveled quietly along my shoulders to both arms. Then it moved to my neck and slowly to my entire head. It traveled all over my body.

After the warmth disappeared, I felt comfortable and relaxed. An extreme peace came upon me and stayed with me. The Lord had granted it. He took all of my anxiety and sorrows away. I felt hot and even began to sweat. I could hardly endure the heat and started to take off my extra clothes. I had dressed in many layers. I wore a scarf over my head, a hat, three wool sweaters, a coat, a thick scarf around my neck, two pairs of trousers (one made of cotton and the other of wool) and another pair of pants, a blanket around my thighs, tall boots, and two pairs of socks. I took off my top layers, removing one piece of clothing after another until only a shirt remained.

I was no longer the same. When I drove down the hill, I rolled down the windows, sang songs, and praised the Lord Jesus, "When I have you, I have light. When I have you, I have direction. You make a way for me in the ocean. You are my harbor. I will look upon you and sing to you forever. You channel a river to me in the desert. You will always be my strength."

I returned home carrying my clothes in my arms. My husband looked at me in a strange way because he didn't know where I had gone or what had happened that morning. With no explanation, I ran quickly into the bedroom and took off the trousers made of cotton and wool. While I was in the car, I could take off the clothes from my upper body but not the pants. I was overcome by the heat. Checking the air temperature, it was seventy-nine degrees Fahrenheit.

My health was restored ever since that very moment. Two months later, I started my first full-time job after coming to the United States, and since then I have never stopped working. Shortly after that, the federal government hired my husband. The wheels of life began to turn again and move forward, yet our lives were never the same because we were closer to the Lord.

Later I understood why Jesus had been silent and had turned His back on me before I was healed. He wanted me to learn to pray for others' salvation, just like He did when He humbly carried the sins of the world on His shoulders and prayed for our lives before the Father. He really is the Son of the Father. He forgives our sins; He is merciful to us and performs miracles for us. With His almighty hand, He touched me, cured me and made me free. He is the God who honors His word. He is the God of healing, and nothing is impossible for Him.

Because of the failure of our financial investments, our life was more limited than before. However, I learned to be thankful in the midst of it, treasure what I owned, share what I had, care for the poor, and be merciful to strangers and the homeless. In our investments, we lost merely money but gained something beyond what money could buy. Money has its price, but Jesus is priceless. Material things cannot bring me to heaven, but that which is priceless can provide me with eternal life.

Our investment failures drew me closer to the Lord. It brought me to the Living Water, to the spiritual storehouses of His provision, and to the words of Jesus Christ, which promises that we will never be hungry or thirsty again.

THE SANCTUARY OF PRAYER

After my healing I started to read the Bible seriously on a daily basis. Soon I felt that reading at home wasn't quite the right situation for me. The phone and the dog's barking often distracted me. So I asked the Lord to show me a place where I could be more focused on studying the Bible. In 2008, Jesus answered my prayer by leading me to a park with a beautiful view, Canyon Park in Monrovia. This park is very quiet in the morning, and it was a perfect place for me. I like to go there to read the Bible before I go to work.

No other book has been so appealing to me or spoken so directly to me like the Bible. The more I read the Bible, the more I can't put it down. I am continually amazed at how true it is. It presents the Lord whom I had seen in my vision but could not describe, in accurate and simple words. In Jesus I finally found all the answers to the questions that had flooded my mind the night I had been saved in the sea at Sanya. Through reading the Bible I learned more about God's holiness, love, integrity, mercy, goodness, kindness and righteousness. The more I learned about Him, the more I was hungry for His Word, and the more I wanted to do something for Him. But there was a big problem standing in the way.

I had frequently asked the Lord: "Jesus, since I came to the United States, I have been to different churches. People have asked me how I came to know you or how I became a Christian. I have wanted to share my testimony, but why can't I do it? I don't even remember how many times I have tried to tell or write down my story. Why, whenever I started to speak about my experience, does my tongue become stiff and I begin to stutter? I have never stuttered when talking about anything else before, so why should I become like this whenever I mention my encounter with you? Why, whenever I start to write down the story, does my thinking go blank, my heart quiver and my body tremble all over, as if a very strong current is going through my body? It has been like this for more than twelve years. I don't understand it. Don't you want your name to be known and glorified?" I asked these questions repeatedly, yet I had no answer.

My friends would say, "Don't worry, it's not God's time yet. You have to wait. Pray about it and we will pray for you too." Three more years passed, and I still didn't get an answer. I was disappointed and frustrated. *How long would I have to wait? Was God still there? Would He listen to my prayer at all?* I wasn't sure. I felt

God had walked away from me. I was filled with anxiety and was a bit depressed. I spiritually became very weak, and started to doubt whether I should continue to spend my time in the park reading His Word or not. I didn't want to waste my time since God had ignored me for so long. However, God had His own way to answer my prayers, and He did it in His own time.

On April 18, 2011, during my regular routine, I drove into the Canyon Park. After passing a small bridge, I turned left and started driving up towards the top of the hill. At that moment, I saw a man walk out from a trail with a cell phone close to his left ear. Following him were four other men and women. I knew this group of "early birds." They often came to this park in the morning, and about the time I drove in, they would be on their way out. We would always meet somewhere on the road. They would smile and joyfully wave to me, and I would do the same to them even though we had never talked to each other. Their open, friendly and happy attitude made me think that they had something very special inside of them, and I wished to have it too.

But on that day, not only did they not wave to me, but they also had very anxious and worried looks on their faces. *Why was that? Had someone been attacked by a bear?* I wondered. I had seen bears several times close to the place where they had just walked out. So I stopped the car and looked back at what was going on. From a distance, I saw that they had walked toward a ranger who was working in the park. They talked to him and pointed to where they had just walked out. Then the ranger immediately left with his truck toward the park entrance. It seemed he was going somewhere to get something for them.

I sensed that something was terribly wrong and reversed the car to get closer to the group. Then I shouted, "What happened? Is there anything I can do for you?"

"Someone collapsed," one of them replied. "Do you have a phone? Mine doesn't work." Before I even understood the last part of his statement, he quickly disappeared with the group into the same trail where they had just walked out.

I jumped out of my car and grabbed a cushion from the back seat. Whoever collapsed needed it in this chilly and damp forest! I followed their trail and very soon caught up with them. They were standing in front of a bench in a semicircle.

As I approached, one of them asked me: "Are you a nurse?"

"No, I'm not, but maybe I can help. May I try?" I answered.

"Yes, please," said one of them.

People automatically moved aside and let me in. In the middle of that semicircle was an aged woman paralyzed on the ground with her husband supporting her back. The woman was breathing very rapidly. Her eyes were half closed, and her face was extremely pale. She was sweating profusely, and her trousers were soiled. Her life was in a very dangerous and threatening situation.

"What happened?" I asked.

Her husband answered, "She was sitting on the bench, but then collapsed. It was a heart attack." He could not speak English, and someone else translated for me.

"We need to place this cushion underneath her. This ground is too cold for her plus it is wet," I said to the husband.

"No, she doesn't want to move," the husband tried to protect his wife. He gently patted her back, and wished his dear one would feel better by him doing so.

"We have to, that will keep her warm. Please, help me," I insisted.

The husband followed then, and I knelt down. We managed to place the cushion under the woman. I touched her forehead and hands; they were very cold. I pulled her left sleeve up to her elbow, selected two acupuncture points and started to press on them. The points were good for heart problems. I had four years of experience in school, clinics and hospitals when I was in China, and I knew exactly how to deal with an emergency case like this.

Everyone kept silent while I was working on the aged woman. I tried my best; however, her situation wasn't getting any better. Her life was fading away in front of our eyes. I heard the people behind me starting to talk to each other in a language that I didn't know. Suddenly, they all knelt down and laid their hands on the woman and on her husband and continued to speak in that language until I heard them all say "Amen." Then I realized they had just prayed for her. They were absolutely right: cell phones don't work in the forest, but Jesus Christ and His Holy Spirit do! Doesn't the Bible say that our

God is a living God, that He never stops working, and that anyone can call on His name anytime, anywhere and in any circumstance!

I was so encouraged and touched. I also closed my eyes and started to pray for the woman in silence while I was holding her hands. "Jesus," I prayed, "save this woman. Holy Spirit, please bring her life back. Satan, leave her. Devil of death, I command you to get out of her in the name of Jesus. Holy Spirit, lift her up. Jesus, your child is ill. Help her; show your power."

Before I finished my prayer, I heard someone saying, "She said she is feeling much better now!" I opened my eyes in awe at what I saw. The aged woman was sitting on the cushion by herself, and her face was returning to normal. Her lips showed red, she stopped sweating, her breath calmed down and she was smiling!

"Yee!" everyone released and clapped their hands. Right at that moment, two paramedic cars arrived with all the necessary equipment. The paramedics immediately started into their duties to take good care of the aged woman. They asked her husband questions, reviewed the medications that he had been carrying for her, and then communicated to doctors through a special line. Then they gave the woman an IV and measured her blood pressure. "Very good, the blood pressure is normal," the paramedic said to us and wrote it down in his report. After that, they took the aged woman to a nearby hospital.

Later on, I learned that the people who had led me to the lady were Korean Presbyterians, and they were just passing by. A week after that, I received a surprise phone call from the aged woman's daughter. She told me that her mom had gone back to her own home happily on that same day. The doctor had checked everything that needed to be checked; yet nothing was abnormal. She thanked me for what I had done to help save her mom's life and said, that because of this incident, she had decided to go back to church, which she hadn't done for a long time. She felt God was calling her back to Himself.

I was so happy to hear that and gave all the praise and thanks to Jesus. I knew that the recovery of this aged woman had nothing to do with me. It was because of those wonderful brothers and sisters who had earnestly pleaded to the Lord for her life. And it was really because of Jesus, my Savior and the Savior of the World. He had listened to those prayers and had responded with a miracle. That reminded me of how my life had been saved in the sea at Sanya because of the Christians in America who had prayed for my salvation.

In both cases, the devil was trying to destroy people's lives, and was trying to make us believe that there was no protection, no hope and that we had to give up. But the devil is a liar and a complete loser. He lost his power when sincere prayers were made to Jesus, the Lamb of God. The devil took off in a flash because he knew Jesus is the Author of Life and the Master of the Universe, and he knew the power of Christ's blood could crush his head. In both cases, the salvation of Christ served as people's shield, fortress, defense, and high tower. And in both cases, the life that the devil was trying to destroy was saved through Jesus Christ. What a true and faithful Savior Jesus is!

I repented and asked the Lord to forgive me for my doubts about Him. I wasn't anxious or depressed any more, and I had learned one of my most valuable lessons in life that day. God doesn't want people to merely read the Bible or write a story about Him. He wants us to pray about everything and to build His new tabernacle on earth within our heart. He wants our hearts to become a house of prayer: a sanctuary, a place where the Holy Spirit dwells. He wants to meet us there, and when He comes, that's the moment that our prayers are answered. He wants us to be guided by Him and live out His words. Then what He teaches us in the Bible will become alive through our actions. When people around us see what we do, they will start to rethink the meaning of life and will want to have a relationship with Christ. In this way, Jesus is glorified.

I realized that I was way behind in what God wanted me to be. I questioned myself as to the real reason why I was coming to the park. Had I just been following my own routine in life, rather than God's? Had I been enjoying the view of the canyon, the hills, the valley, the grass, the trees and everything in it more than the One who put them all there? Had I been praying a lot, yet actually nagging and complaining more than praising and thanking Him? Had I been asking to receive rather than giving? After some reflecting, I realized that I wanted things to be done in my way rather than His. I had been putting myself first rather than Him. I had been reading the Bible, yet without really seeking the meaning of the words. I had made His Word, the precious source of life, become useless like a dry well. I had been calling Him Lord, yet not making Him Lord. I had been spending time in the park, yet not worshiping the true God.

I confessed and started to ask the Lord to show me how to be a true worshiper of Him. I spent more time reading Psalms and praying, and I came to understand that previously I hadn't been ready to write this story. Since the day I was saved by the Lord in the sea at Sanya, fifteen years had passed. During these years, Jesus has given me many assignments. I learned that I must be disciplined, I must deal with weakness, be put through brokenness, and accept failures. I learned that I must grow, become strong, be built up, and remember the lessons I'd learned. I had to understand the value of waiting, the power of prayer and the meaning of humility. I had to learn how to repent, to be grateful, and to be thankful. I had to read the Bible more and praise Him continuously. Only then could I write down this story about Him.

I wasn't sure when that day would finally arrive, but I had stopped asking the Lord when I should speak out or write down my story, and I stopped trying to do it in my own way. If God wasn't in it, then anything I did would be in vain. I learned to make my heart a sanctuary of prayer, and I asked my friends to join me in a new prayer for God's guidance. If necessary, I was willing to wait for another fifteen years or even longer than that before I would write my story down.

God has a tender heart and a sense of humor. He forgave me everything that I had done wrong and only had me wait for three more years. Then His Holy Spirit began to work in me. He made my hands His hands. When I sat in front of the computer, I wasn't the one writing, but He was. He brought my mind back to the moment when He appeared to me in Sanya in the sea, so that I could clearly explain how I experienced Him. Because of His constant inspiration, I have been able to write my story and share it with others.

Chapter 20

JESUS CHRIST IS CALLING US

Although eighteen years have passed since I was saved in the sea of Sanya. I still clearly remember how I was with Christ in my vision, how I saw His precious blood, how I heard His unforgettable voice, how I experienced His incredible love. His love expressed through His blood and calling are so real, giving, and persistent that it deeply touches my soul, all the time.

How I thank Jesus! I would have no life without Christ my Savior. Jesus is the God of not only the Jews but also the Gentiles. He loves not only His chosen people but also the nobodies like me who have nothing. He is the God of all! He loves every one of us and each life that He created on the earth. Because of His love, I had converted from being an atheist to being a follower of Christ. I went from doing wrong things to walking on the right path, from being a spiritual vagrant to being an heir of His kingdom, and from being a prodigal to being a child of Almighty God.

In my vision, heaven spoke, "My child, you have come back at last. I have been waiting for you for so long!" This voice echoed all around me and aroused me from my ignorance. How sinful I was! For many years, I had refused to know Him, yet He had been waiting for me. I ignored Him for no reason, yet He called me His child. I was caught in adultery, yet He forgave all my trespasses. I requested to die as a sinner, yet He had mercy on me and gave me a second life. I waited to be taken to hell, yet He welcomed me back to my real home.

This voice has been lingering in my ears ever since then, and I can never forget the way He lovingly spoke to me. In fact, what the Lord spoke to me was not merely for me, but is for all the people in the world. We are all His children. Jesus is waiting for us. He is calling us to look for Him, to know Him, to accept Him, to trust Him. He is calling us to confess our sins and repent and to come back to His arms.

I once had a chance to share my story with an Iranian friend of mine. I didn't expect that my story would have so much impact on her. She was deeply touched by the power of the Holy Spirit while I was talking that tears began to roll down her cheeks. Later, I gave her a Bible as a gift and suggested that she read the New Testament in order to find out the truth. She accepted the Bible and said that she would compare this book with the Koran. I said to her, "I'm glad you are doing this, you will find that only one book tells the truth. Feel free to compare Jesus to Allah to see who truly portrays God. I am sure you will find the answer." I understood how difficult it was for a Muslim to accept Jesus as their Lord, yet I also believed that anyone who was willing to open his or her heart and search for the truth could find Him. All I needed to do was to pray for her and trust God would do the rest.

One late afternoon a few months later I saw her again. She was in tears and told me how she almost died that morning. She left home to go to work very early as usual. Shortly after she was on the freeway, a dense smoke suddenly rose from the front of her car. She smelled burning gasoline and felt that her car could explode at any time in the middle of the traffic. She was very afraid; nevertheless, she managed to change lanes, pull her car off the freeway, and parked on the side of the road. She ran out of her car, called AAA, and rented another car to go to work. By the time she arrived at her office, it was three o'clock in the afternoon.

I could tell she hadn't recovered from this horrible experience. She was exhausted and worried how much it would cost to fix her car. She wept in front of me. Her tears reminded me how I cried at the top of my voice before the Lord in my vision, and how the Lord embraced and comforted me. I decided to pass on the love I had received from Christ to her. I invited her come to my office after she finished her work. I wanted to pray for her before she went home that day.

She hesitated for a bit then accepted my invitation and showed up in my office when the night fell. Three office cleaners were on duty making a huge noise with their vacuums. I brought her to a small room at the back of the office and shut the door to separate us from the noise. The next half hour was going to be time with Jesus Christ and His Holy Spirit. We must not have any interference.

I sat down with my friend face-to-face. Before I even started to talk, she immediately held my hands and asked me to pray for her. She came with such a hungry heart and burning desire in the depth of her soul. She wanted something different in her life and she could not wait. It was very clear that the Spirit of Christ had been calling her since the time I shared my story and gave her the Bible, and now the Almighty God purposely brought her to my office after her car broke down on the freeway that morning. I knew that when the Holy Spirit is working, no one can resist Him. I laid my hands on her head, and led her in a prayer of repentance. She trembled with fear, confessed her sins with tears, and accepted Jesus Christ as her Lord and Savior.

We began to talk. She asked me why she didn't have peace before this, even though she prayed multiple times each day. I asked her in whose name she prayed. She said she prayed in the name of Allah, Muhammad, Moses, David and Jesus. I told her I only pray to God in the name of Jesus; and I reminded her how I was saved by that precious name. Then I told her the Bible says that our God is a jealous God; He doesn't share His glory with other gods. Salvation is found in no one else, "for there is no other name under heaven given to men by which we must be saved". (Acts 4:12) My friend responded, "I want this Jesus! I want to accept Him as my Lord!" Her eyes were sparking with delight.

When we walked outside the office building, my friend gave me a beautiful smile and said that she felt that the moon was bigger than usual and the streetlights were brighter than before. The heavy burden that had been pressing on her heart was taken away. She was amazed that a prayer of confession and a decision to believe in Jesus could make such a big difference in her life. She got into her car with a joy and peace that she never had before and drove away with the Lord's good promises and rich blessings.

I am wondering, how many of us pray many times each day, read religious books and search for God. We should ask ourselves whether we have found an intimate relationship with God, just like the relationship between a father and his children. Have we found abounding love, mercy, grace, kindness and forgiveness? Have we found real joy and peace? Where are our lives heading after we finish our journey on earth? The way to heaven is a narrow way, have we found it yet? If we haven't found the answers for these questions, then I encourage us to read the Gospels and look at Jesus' life, the Messiah and Son of God, and listen to His words. I hope we will hear Jesus' calling, quickly change our life's direction and come to His throne to take the free gift of eternal life.

Dear friends, there are many women who are called "mother" in the world, but there is only one who gave us birth–our biological mother. There are also many false gods who are called "the Lord," but there is only One who created us, and that is Jesus Christ, the only living God. As our Creator, He knows every pathway of our body's blood vessels. He watches every throb of our pulse. He hears each sound of our breath. His heart accords with ours, and He feels what we feel. We all need Him! At this moment, we need His love and mercy, His forgiveness and salvation, and His help and guidance. We need Him to hold our hands as we go through our lives, just like a loving father who holds his children's hands.

Jesus Christ is "the radiance of God's glory and the exact representation of His being." (Heb. 1:3) He is the life, the truth, and the way. Only by recognizing Him can we have hope. Only by accepting Him can we have eternal life. Only by having faith in Him can we go to heaven. Jesus is not far away but rather close to us. He is not in any lifeless religion, handmade temples, or spiritless idols. He is alive! He is in our mouth and in our heart. He is calling us to call upon His name to be saved. Through Him, we can gain hope, receive life, have His abundant grace and salvation! Through Him, we have an opportunity to go to heaven and enjoy the everlasting life.

Dear friend, Jesus Christ is calling us to be with Him in paradise for eternity when we finish our journey on earth. My beloved, Jesus Christ is calling us. Have we heard Him?

Chapter 21

HEAVEN—THE REAL HOME

One day, several years after I came to Los Angeles, I was sitting next to my dining room table and sorting out old photos when I came across a few pictures taken on Sanya Beach. It reminded me of how I had miraculously survived. I looked closer at the photos. I was very young then. As for the man who saved me, I wasn't sure if he still lived in Sanya. I wanted to visit him if I had a chance. In one of the photos, I am wearing a hat and sunglasses. Next to me is the lifeguard. We are standing in the shadows. That's because I was so afraid of the light after seeing the true light of Jesus. My eyes hurt, and I was in tears. I am smiling in the picture, but only I knew it was a bitter smile, and behind that smile was a deep fear.

I glanced at the T-shirt I was wearing, and the old Sanya scene quickly flashed into my mind. I could almost see the blue sky again with the white clouds floating in the air and the rows of tall palm trees swaying in the sea breeze. I could almost hear the sounds again of the waves and children's naive play. Even though everything was gone, I could see it all as if it were yesterday. How could I forget?

When I was just about to gather all the photos and put them away, a pattern and a line of words attracted my attention. I saw a row of palm trees and the English words under it, "Los Angeles." Oh my! Am I not living in the city of Los Angeles? Isn't Los Angeles full of rows of palm trees? I could not believe my eyes.

It was on the new T-shirt that I was wearing in the photo, which Bert had purchased because he liked the words "Los Angeles." After I had put it on, he said to me, "Perhaps you will live in Los Angeles someday. It is a very beautiful city." At that time, I didn't even know where Los Angeles was, much less that one day I really would cross the Pacific Ocean and settle here. Nor could I imagine that seven years after the Lord had saved me, I would be looking at those pictures in my own home in Los Angeles.

On the day that I was looking at the photos, it dawned on me that it had been God's purpose to bring me to Los Angeles. He had hidden His purpose in this picture, waiting for me to discover it by myself. It was one more announcement from the Most High that nothing is a coincidence. There is never a coincidence. Everything was prearranged and planned for me to know Him, accept Him, trust Him, worship Him, praise Him, and proclaim Him so that through me people would know there is no one like Him in the whole world.

Before I was born, I didn't know of His existence, but He prepared nourishment for me through my mother's womb and waited for me to be born. After I was born, I refused to recognize His existence, but He had prepared salvation for me through His crucifixion. When I was in Chengdu, I worried about life. I worried about what to eat, how to clothe myself, and where to live, but in Los Angles, the Lord already had abundantly prepared everything for all my daily needs. Over those years He had patiently waited beside me helping and guiding me until I finally reached this land He had promised me.

I see now that I wasn't wearing an ordinary T-shirt on that day but rather a promise and a mission from the Lord. The story had started in Sanya, China, and now was continuing in Los Angeles, United States of America. For me, this is another sign that God's words are true. When He says something, it will happen and it will be fulfilled! If God could fulfill His words to me by bringing me to Los Angeles, won't He fulfill His promises that He makes to all of us?

Since I was given this mission, I must tell the world how I saw Jesus Christ coming to me from heaven in His glory. He revealed Himself to me who knew nothing about Him at the time. He shed His blood for us—the sinners of the world. Then He went back to heaven in His glory.

The Bible says that before leaving the world, Jesus said to His disciples, "In my Father's house are many rooms;" "I am going there to prepare a place for you. And if I go and prepare a place for you, I will come back and take you to be with me that you also may be where I am." (John 14: 2–3) Do you see? God has prepared a place for us. That place is our resting place and permanent residence, and it will never perish. The gate of that place is open to welcome all the people of the world who are willing to accept Jesus Christ as their Savior.

When our traveling days on earth come to the end, that residence is the destiny of our souls and the place where our life continues. That place is called heaven. Heaven is beautiful and real. Our Lord Jesus Christ is there. His promise is true. He said, "In a little while you will see me no more, and then after a little while you will see me." (John 16:16) That was His word to all who really love Him, fear Him, worship Him, and do His will. Yes, Jesus is waiting for us in heaven, no matter if we are male or female, young or old, Asian or European, African or American.

If one day someone asks me again what my biggest dream is, I will answer without any hesitation, "To go to heaven!" I'm not talking about the place in my dreams, but the veritable heaven — the place that Jesus has provided for us. "Can you tell me why?" that person may ask. Then I will say, "Because Jesus has authority in heaven. In His place, there is love, holiness, and praise. There is no more night or darkness, only glory and true light. There is no more pain and grief, only joy and laughter. There is no more medicine because there is no illness. Nothing needs to be hidden because everything is transparent. Nothing needs to be stored because all things have already been prepared."

Dear friend, why are you still wandering? Aren't you tired yet? Do you desire rest? Come, let's go searching for Jesus and have rest in Him. Jesus is waiting for us. By the door inlaid with pearls, on the street paved with gold, in the river shining like crystal, under the tree bearing fruit monthly, inside the city of His splendor, and before the throne of His glory, Jesus waits for us, longs for us, and calls us to come home.

Heaven is our home—the home of peace, the home of joy, the home of eternity, the only home, and the real home.

CPSIA information can be obtained at www.ICGtesting.com
Printed in the USA
LVOW11s0214100516

487463LV00002B/168/P